LOCATING
UNION &
CONFEDERATE
RECORDS

LOCATING

UNION &

CONFEDERATE

RECORDS

A Guide to the Most Commonly Used Civil War Records
of the National Archives and Family History Library

NANCY JUSTUS MOREBECK

HeritageQuest®, from ProQest Company • North Salt Lake, Utah • 2001

HeritageQuest®, from ProQuest Company
P.O. Box 540670, North Salt Lake, Utah 84054-0670
HeritageQuest is a registered trademark of ProQuest Information and Learning Company.

Printed in the United States of America
05 04 03 02   5 4 3

ISBN (softbound): 0-944931-89-8
ISBN (hardbound): 0-944931-90-1

Contents

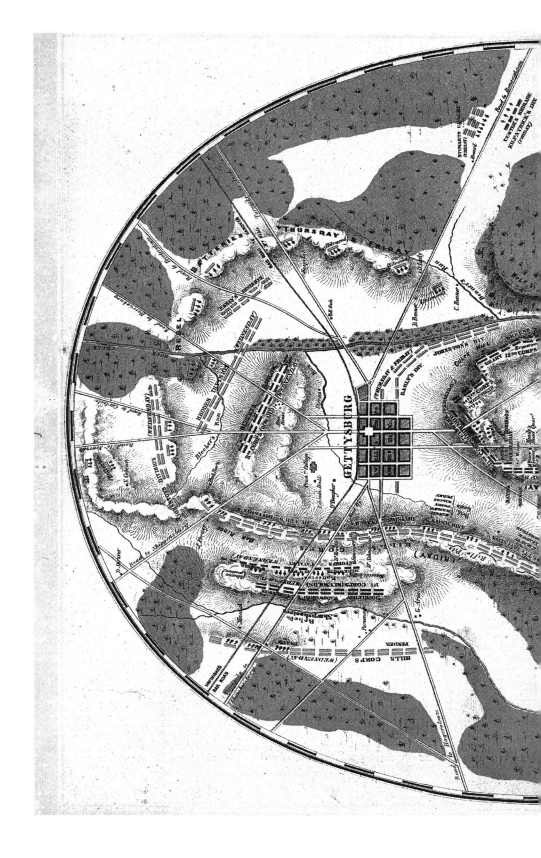

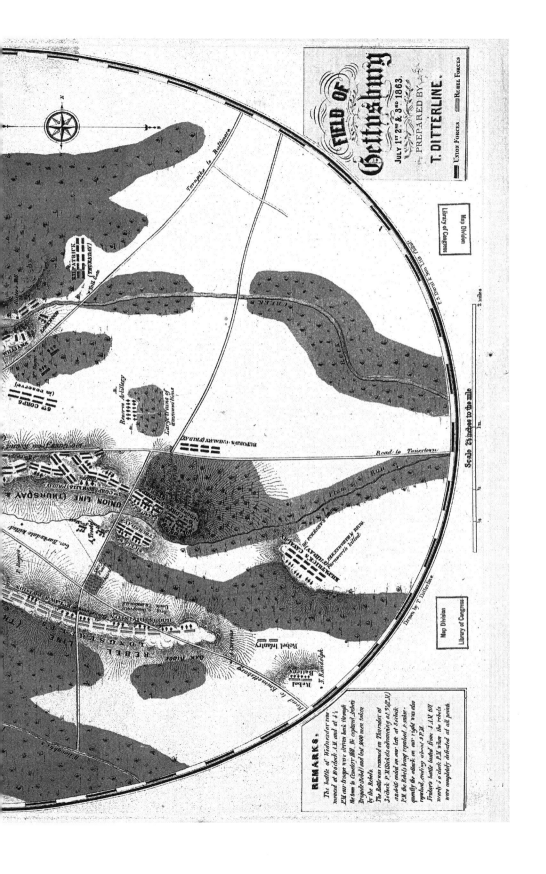

FIELD OF Gettysburg

JULY 1ST 2ND & 3RD 1863.

PREPARED BY

T. DITTERLINE.

UNION FORCES ▬▬▬   REBEL FORCES ▨▨▨

Map Division
Library of Congress

T. N. Persil & Son LITH. PHILAD.

Scale 2⅓ inches to the mile

2 miles

Map Division
Library of Congress

Drawn by T. Ditterline

REMARKS.

The battle of Wednesday commenced at Oclock A.M. and at 4½ P.M. our troops were driven back through the town to Cemetery Hill. We captured Archers Brigade dead and lost 5000 men taken by the Rebels.

The battle was renewed on Thursday at 3oclock P.M.Kickels skirmishing at 5½ P.M. and the attack on our left at 5oclock P.M. the Rebels being repulsed, & subsequently the attack on our right was also repulsed, ceasing about 8 P.M.

Friday's battle lasted from 4 A.M. till nearly 6 oclock P.M. when the rebels were completely defeated at all points.

Turnpike to Baltimore

KILPATRICK

(THURSDAY)

DUCK CREEK

RUN

6TH CORPS (IN RESERVE)

Reserve Artillery

Large trains of ammunitions

BUFORDS CAVALRY (FRIDAY)

Road to Taneytown

Plum Run

UNION LINE (THURSDAY)

MERRICK'S CAVALRY (THURSDAY)

MERRICK'S CAVALRY Worthworth killed

Gen. Barksdale killed

REBEL LINE LONGSTREET'S

Rebel Infantry

Rebel Battery

J. R. Randolph

Road to Emmettsburg

Gettysburg, Pa. The cemetery gatehouse. *1863 July.*
Library of Congress, Prints & Photographs Division (LC-B8171-2388)

(Overleaf) Field of Gettysburg, July 1st, 2nd & 3rd, 1863 Prepared by
T. Ditterline. *Philada. P. S. Duval & Son lith., 1863. Library of Congress,
Geography and Map Division (G3824.G3S5 1863 .D42 CW 331)*

Introduction

Searching for Information on Your Civil War Soldier

So, Grandpa, or Great-grandpa served during the Civil War. Where do I find the records? Where do I find the unit in which Grandpa served? This book will help the family historian or genealogist to track down those elusive records and put some interesting information on your ancestor into the family history. Follow the steps below to find the military unit your soldier served in as a Union Volunteer or Confederate Soldier.

Union

The fastest way to find the military unit your soldier served in is by using *The Roster of Union Soldiers*. This new publication lists the soldier's name and the unit he was in from the entries of the National Archives' Union Compiled Military Service Records. Remember this source is for Union Volunteers, not Regular Army enlisted men as the *Compiled Military Service Records* are for Volunteer Soldiers only. Using *The Roster of Union Soldiers* helps one rapidly find the unit in which the soldier served. One must first know the *state* under which the soldier volunteered, as the records are compiled by state, then alphabetically by name. This set of books states the unit in which your ancestor served. The book is available at the LDS Family History Library and should be available at other large archives and libraries.

Hewett, Janet B., editor. *The Roster of Union Soldiers.* Wilmington, NC: Broadfoot Publishing Co., 1998. 33 Volumes.

Confederate

The fastest way to find the military unit a Confederate soldier served in is by using *The Roster of Confederate Soldiers 1861-1865,* which has copied the entries of names and units found in the National Archives' Confederate Compiled Military Service Records. This is a consolidated index to all States' Confederate soldiers. One does not need to know the state under which he served; all names are in an alphabetical listing. If he has a common surname, knowing the state he served from will help. The Roster gives the military unit in which the soldier served. It is available at the Family History Library and at California State Library, Sutro Branch, San Francisco, California. It should also be available at other large archives and libraries. This is the easiest way to find the unit in which your Confederate soldier was enrolled.

Hewett, Janet B., editor. *The Roster of Confederate Soldiers 1861-1865,*Wilmington, N.C.: Broadfoot Publishing Co., 1996. 16 Volumes.

Union or Confederate?

If unable to locate your ancestor in the above two listed sets of books, do the following steps to find his unit.

Check with other relatives who might have the information.

Check his gravestone; military information is sometimes included.

Check the office records of the cemetery where he is interred.

Check his newspaper obituary; again the military unit may be stated.

Check for a local county history (Biographical Sketch Book) *where he was living after the Civil War* for a biographical sketch written about him in which he would be proud to have his military service listed.

Check for a county history (Biographical Sketch Book) where he was *residing during the civil war*. The county histories usually have sections on the military history of their county and often list the men who served in the units from their county.

Check the Federal Census of 1860 for the State of residence if you do not know the county where your ancestor was residing. For 1860 there are "Head of Household Census Indexes" both in books and on CD-ROMs.

Check the 1890 Veteran's Census for a veteran from states Kentucky through Wyoming for data on your Civil War ancestor if he lived until 1890. This will state the military unit in which he served.

Check a State Census if one is available in the state in which your ancestor resided after his military service. The state censuses often denote the military unit in which he served.

The Homestead Act (passed by Congress in 1862) allowed a settler to obtain legal ownership of a tract of land (usually 160 acres) by occupying it for five years and making improvements to the land. Congress gave increasingly generous homestead rights to Union Civil War veterans. Eventually, a Union veteran could get as much as three years' credit for time spent in the military applied to the five year homestead period. The widows and orphans of Union soldiers were also entitled to special treatment. The homestead application of the soldier, his widow, or his orphans may contain proof of his military service possibly even including his original discharge papers. Once you have obtained the legal description of the land, obtain the patent number from the deed or from the Bureau of Land Management, then get the Homestead File using NATF Form 84 from the National Archives.

Checklist—You Have the Military Unit, What Next?

You can now check many of the records listed below to find information about your ancestor's involvement in the Civil War. A list follows on some of the records that are covered in this book. The record types covered are not all the records that are available in searching for Civil War soldier data. The records are arranged in a type of time line for the soldiers involvement in the military service to his Union or his Confederate units.

Enlistments Regular Army, Union & Confederate Volunteers

Conscription Records—Union and some Confederate

Compiled Military Service Records—Union or Confederate

Officers of Union and Confederate Armies

Compiled Records Showing Service of Military Units—
Union or Confederate

Regimental Histories

Union Prison Records

Confederate Prison Records

Pension Files—Union or Confederate

Confederate Amnesty Papers

Soldiers' Homes

Veteran Organizations

Union Deaths and Burials

Confederate Deaths and Burials

Finding Aids:

National Archives & Branch Archive Addresses

Addresses of Libraries and Archives

Federal Census of 1890, Veterans and Widows

Federal Census of 1910

State Censuses

Civil War Web Sites

Washington, D.C. Six marines with fixed bayonets at the Navy Yard. *1864 April.*
Library of Congress, Prints & Photographs Division (LC-B8171-7697)

1

Enlistment Records— Regular Army, Union & Confederate Volunteers

Regular Army Enlistment Records (M233)

Please note these records are Regular Army and most of those who served during the Civil War were from Volunteer Units. Union enrollments were approximated at 2,000,000 volunteer troops and 67,000 regulars. At the time of the Civil War, the Regular Army had 15,000 Officers and men. The Officer Corps was torn apart by resignation of it's members to support the Confederacy while the vast majority of the enlisted regular soldiers remained loyal to the Army of the Union. Enlistment records are grouped by date of enlistment and then alphabetically by the soldier's name. The records give the following information: Name; Rank; Regiment; Company commander; Regimental commander; Height; Weight; Color of eyes, hair, complexion; Age; Occupation; County and state of birth; Date and place of enlistment; Miscellaneous remarks. This record group is very important as there are no Compiled Military Service Records for the Regular Army enlisted men.

ENLISTMENT YEARS	NATIONAL ARCHIVES ROLLS M233*	FHL MICROFILM #
1859-1863 A-K	27	350333
1859-1863 L-Z	28	350334
1864-1865 A-K	29	350335
1864-1865 L-Z	30	350336

*To order HeritageQuest films in Series M233 see chapter 22.

Volunteer Enlistment—Union and Confederate

For the volunteers who served in the Civil War most states both Union and Confederate had enrollment or enlistment records which were compiled by the State's Adjutant General. The records were sometimes published in book form and are available at the Family History Library in Salt Lake and other large genealogical libraries and state archives. The large volumes were often published in the late 1860's, after the Civil War. In the book format, the information included is abbreviated from the original enrollment lists. Listed is Name, Residence or Quota, Date of Muster, Term of Service, Regiment or Corps, and Where Mustered. To find the original rolls of the State's Regiments, microfilm copies may also be available and can be located using the Family History Library Catalog: [State] - [Military] - [Civil War] - [Records] using the name of the state you are researching or possibly even by [State] - [Military]. The author of the record is the State Adjutant General. The information stated on the original enlistment records includes: Name, Rank, Date of enlistment; Place of enlistment; by Whom enlisted; Term of enlistment; and Residence. This information is much the same as contained in the Compiled Military Service Record's Company Descriptive Book and Company Muster Roll which is included when you send for the Compiled Military Service Record from the National Archives. The Compiled Military Service Records includes a brief physical descripton of the soldier which includes: Age, Height, Complexion, Eyes, Where Born, and Occupation. The enlistment records *may* list the town rather than the county where the soldier was born.

Regular U.S. Army Enlistment (not volunteers) Record. *Microfilm no. 350335, Family History Library, Salt Lake City, Utah.*

Petersburg, Va. Two youthful military telegraph operators at headquarters. *1864 August. Library of Congress, Prints & Photographs Division (LC-B8171-1025)*

2

Union
Draft Records

The first national draft in U.S. history was signed by President Lincoln with the Enrollment Act on March 3, 1863. It was created to supply men to fight for the Union as the number of volunteers continued to dwindle. The length of the war, severity of wounds, and care of the wounded all contributed to the lack of volunteerism. Under the new draft bill, all eligible males between the ages of 20 and 45, both white citizens and aliens, who had declared their intent to naturalize, were eligible for the draft. Males 20 to 35 were to be drafted first, followed by all married men between the ages of 36 to 46. Males ages 17 to 20 could serve with the consent of their parent of guardian. The records of the draft include men born between 1818 and 1843 who did not serve as well as those who served in the Army during the Civil War. The draft applied only to men residing in states of the United States under Union control. Five record types have been used by historians and genealogists and are discussed below.

Consolidated Lists

Consolidated Lists are the draft registration records which resulted from the Civil War draft. All males between the ages of 18 and 45 who were residing in Union states were to sign up. The Consolidated Lists can provide useful data on males born between 1818 and 1843. Information requested of draft-eligible men found in the Consolidated Lists include full

Locating Union and Confederate Records

TABLE II.—CONSOLIDATED LIST of all persons of Class II, subject to do military duty in the _Eighth_ Congressional District, consisting of the ~~Counties of~~ _Smith_ _Fifteenth_ and _Sixteenth Wards city_ State of _New York_ enumerated during the month of _May & June_, 186_3_, under direction of _Captain James G. Fox_, Provost Marshal.

RESIDENCE	NAME	Age 1st July, 1863.	White or Colored.	PROFESSION, OCCUPATION, or TRADE.	PLACE OF BIRTH. (Naming the State, Territory, or Country.)	FORMER MILITARY SERVICE.	REMARKS	
8º Ave	Northrope William	44	W	Confectiony	New York			1
West 38ª St	Northrop Levi M	40	W	Lawyer	Conn			2
Yard Fort 3d	Neil Henry	44	W	Laborer				3
West 18º St	Need James	42	W	Cabinet maker	Ireland			4
West 36 St	Nolan Daniel	44	W	Gas meters	Ireland			5
West 18º St	Noble James	43	W	Wailer	Ireland			6
West 21º St	Nettleton Horace	38	W	Jeweller	New York			7
West 24º St	Nodine Philip	44	W	Stage driver	New York			8
West 18º St	Northoren Thomas	38	W	Mineral water	England			9
West 34º St	Niblo James P	44	W	Mason	New Jersey			10
West 15º St	Nulle Louis	44	W	Fresco paint	Germany			11
9th Avenue	Newson William	40	W	Broker	New Jersey			12
West 33º St	Northrop Wm B	44	W	Merchant	New York			13
West 34 St	Norman John H	38	W	Paper hangs	England			14
West 30 St	Nelson Zachariah	42	W	Clerk	New York			15
9º Ave	Northropd Hector	46	W	Shoe maker	New York			16
W 33d & N Av	Norton George	36	W	Jeweller	Conn			17
West 18º St	Norman George	42	W	Carpenter	Scotland			18
West 19º St	Neagle James	44	W	Porter	Ireland			19
Eighth Ave	Nicholson Hester C	40	W	Broker	New York			20

Colonel JAMES B. FRY,
Provost Marshal General U.S.
Washington, D.C.

STATION: Headquarter _Eighth_ Congr. Dist. of _New York_
DATE: _1st July 1863_

Provost Marshal

Example from Consolidated Lists. _Courtesy of the National Archives._

name, place of residence, age, occupation, marital status, place of birth, and prior military service. The Consolidated Lists are contained in Record Group 110 at the National Archives and Records Administration I and are available by mail request from the National Archives and Records Administration. It is necessary to provide the Archives with the Congressional District in which the male was residing at the time. *An example of a page of a Consolidated List is on the previous page.*

Medical Records of Examinations

Medical Records of Examinations are organized by state and then by Congressional District. They are the records of men drafted or rejected and are also part of Record Group 110 held at the National Archives and Records Administration I. Data includes: name, residence, age, place of birth, occupation, physical characteristics, accepted or rejected, and remarks. If a man was rejected due to a medical reason, his disability would have been listed in the Medical Records of Examinations. This record group is not available by mail request. It is necessary to know the Congressional District where the male was residing and this record group can accessed by doing one's own research or by hiring a researcher in the Washington D.C. area.

Descriptive Rolls

Descriptive Rolls were created when the male was drafted. They serve to identify the male by a personal description, exact place of birth, and whether accepted or rejected for service. They include the following categories: name, place of residence, age, occupation, marital status, place of birth, prior military service, personal description, accepted or rejected. The place of birth is by *County of State* or *County of Country* which is very helpful in the search for place of birth. The Descriptive Rolls are part of Record Group 110 at the National Archives and Records Administration I, and are not available by mail request. It is necessary to know the Congressional District where the male was residing. *An example of two pages of a Descriptive Roll follows.*

Descriptive Roll of Drafted Men

DESCRIPTION.

NO.	NAMES.	AGE.	EYES.	HAIR.	COMPLEXION	HEIGHT.		WHERE BORN.		OCCUPATION
						Feet.	Inches.	State or Kingdom.	Town or County.	

3rd Cong'l 1st Dist. 1 & 2 Eck

1	Isaac D. Gregg	40	Grey	Dark	Light	5	7	Penna	Chester Co	Carp
2	Thomas Festo	21	Grey	Dark	Dark	5	1	Penna	Chester	Print
3	J. James Belt	32	Hazel	Blk	Light	5	9	Delaware	NewCastle	Engine
4	Hartman Wreen	21	Hazel	Dark	Light	5	9½	Germany		Cooper
5	Sampson Cook	45	Grey	Light	Light	5	7½	England	Central	Paint
6	Patrick Monnahan	32	Blue	Light	Light	5	6	Ireland		Butcher
7	Henry Wolfe									
8	Thomas Harrison	24		Light	Light	5	5	England	Derbsh	Labr
9	Samuel Curry	39	Blue	Sandy	Light	6	½	Ireland	Antrim	Tennant
10	Christopher Braken	36	Hazel	Dark	Dark	5	10	Germany		Blksmith
11	James McIntire	26		Light	Light	5	5	Ireland	Donegal	Labr
12	William Bond	30		Blue	Dark	5	10	Ireland	Down Co	Coachm
13	James Connelly	24		Blk	Light	5	6	England		Bricklr
14	Samuel W. Relins	22	Hazel	Sandy	Light	5	3	Delaware	Wilming	Jeweler
15	Nicholas L. Gonnan	33	Blue	Brown	Light			Britian	Mary	Print
16	Enoch Stotsenburg	30		Dark	Light	5	6	Delaware	Wilming	Ironfdr
17	John McGovern	30	Hazel	Dark	Light	5	8	Ireland	Derry Co	Laborer
18	George Freeman	26		Light	Light	5	7½	Germany	Bremen	Clerk
19	Joseph Montgomery	22	Blue	Brown	Light	5	7	Ireland	Donegal	Car
20	Joseph H. Sheppard	27		Brown	Light	5	5	Delaware	NewCastle	Mill
21	Charles M. Allmond	42	Hazel	Dark	Dark	5	8½	Delaware	NewCastle	Hotel Kp
22	Robert Fist	37	Hazel	Light	Fair	5	11	Germany	Wortmn	Labr
23	Patrick Dougherty	26	Hazel	Sandy	Dark	5	6	Ireland	Donegal	Labr
24	John Saunders	37	Blue	Dark	Light	5	4	Ireland	Dublin	Laborer
25	Robert Royal									
26	Edwin Enfield	46	Hazel	Brown	Dark	5	7	Penna	Chester Co	Glassm
27	Francis Snicler	52	Hazel	Dark	Dark	5	10	Penna	Morris Co	Hom Pr
28	Hezekiah Hoops	32	Blue	Dark	Light	5	9	Penna	Chester	Clerk
29	Andrew J. Morgan	27	Hazel	Dark	Light	5	10	Delaware	NewCastle	Paint
30	John Donnahoe	25	Blue	Dark	Light	5	5	Ireland	Devon	Mer
31	Augustine Sane	20	Blue	Light	Light	5	13½	Delaware	Wil	Vol
32	David H. Eston	36		Dark	Light	5	8	New Jersey	Lolventr	Saloon
33	Joseph D. Palmer	35	Brown	Dark	Dark	5	6½	Germany		Morclr
34	Peter Springer	43	Grey	Dark	Light	5	8½	Delaware	NewCastle	Saloon

Example from Descriptive Rolls. *Courtesy of the National Archives.*

Called into the Service of the United States.

ENROLLED.		DRAFTED.			
WHEN.	WHERE.	WHEN.	WHERE.		REMARKS.
June 1863	3ᵈ Ward 1ˢᵗ Prect	May 1864	June 1ˢᵗ 1864	X	Paid Commutation money
June 1863	3ᵈ Ward 1ˢᵗ Prect	May 1864	June 1ˢᵗ 1864		Exempt on Physical Disability
June 1863	3ᵈ Ward 1ˢᵗ Prect	May 1864	June 1ˢᵗ 1864	X	Paid Commutation money
June 1863	3ᵈ Ward 1 Prect	May 1864	June 1ˢᵗ 1864	X	Exempt New residence
June 1863	3ᵈ Ward 1 Prect	May 1864	June 1ˢᵗ 1864		Exempt on Physical Disability
June 1863	3ᵈ Ward 1 Prect	May 1864	June 4ᵗʰ 1864	X	Paid Commutation
June 1863	3ᵈ Ward 1 Prect	May 1864	June 1ˢᵗ 1864	X	Exempt on age
June 1863	3ᵈ Ward 1 Prect	May 1864	June 1ˢᵗ 1864	X	Paid Commutation money
June 1863	3ᵈ Ward 1 Prect	May 1864	June 1ˢᵗ 1864		Exempt Physical Disability
June 1863	3ᵈ Ward 1 Prect	May 1864	June 1ˢᵗ 1864	X	Exempt on age
June 1863	3ᵈ Ward 1 Prect	May 1864	June 1ˢᵗ 1864	X	Paid Commutation money
June 1863	3ᵈ Ward 1 Prect	May 1864	June 1ˢᵗ 1864	X	Exempt on age
June 1863	3ᵈ Ward 1 Prect	May 1864	June 6ᵗʰ 1864	X	Paid Commutation
June 1863	3ᵈ Ward 1 Prect	May 1864	June 3ᵈ 1863	X	Paid Commutation money
June 1863	3ᵈ Ward 1 Prect	May 1864	June 1ˢᵗ 1864	X	Paid Commutation money
June 1863	3ᵈ Ward 1 Prect	May 1864	June 1ˢᵗ 1864		Exempt on Physical Disability
June 1863	3ᵈ Ward 1 Prect	May 1864	June 1ˢᵗ 1864	X	Exempt on age
June 1863	3ᵈ Ward 1 Prect	May 1864	June 1ˢᵗ 1864	X	Exempt on age
June 1863	3ᵈ Ward 1 Prect	May 1864	June 4 1864		Exempt on Physical Disability
June 1863	3ᵈ Ward 1 Prect	May 1864	June 7ᵗʰ 1864	X	Paid Commutation money
June 1863	3ᵈ Ward 1 Prect	May 1864	June 1ˢᵗ 1864		Exempt on Physical Disability
June 1863	3ᵈ Ward 1 Prect	May 1864	June 1ˢᵗ 1864		Exempt on Physical Disability
June 1863	3ᵈ Ward 1 Prect	May 1864	June 1ˢᵗ 1864	X	Paid Commutation money
June 1863	3ᵈ Ward 1 Prect	May 1864	June 1ˢᵗ 1864	X	Exempt on age
June 1863	3ᵈ Ward 1 Prect	May 1864	June 1ˢᵗ 1864	X	Paid Commutation money
June 1863	3ᵈ Ward 1 Prect	May 1864	June 1ˢᵗ 1864		Exempt on Physical Disability
June 1863	3ᵈ Ward 1 Prect	May 1864	June 6ᵗʰ 1864		Exempt on Physical Disability
June 1863	3ᵈ Ward 1 Prect	May 1864	June 1ˢᵗ 1864	X	Paid Commutation money
June 1863	3ᵈ Ward 1 Prect	May 1864	June 1 1864	X	Paid Commutation money
June 1863	3ᵈ Ward 1 Prect	May 1864	June 1ˢᵗ 1864		Exempt on Physical Disability
June 1863	3ᵈ Ward 1 Prect	May 1864	June 1ˢᵗ 1864	X	Paid Commutation money
June 1863	3ᵈ Ward 1 Prect	May 1864	June 1ˢᵗ 1864		Exempt on Physical Disability

Statement of Substitutes

Statement of Substitutes were created from lists of men who were paid to substitute for a drafted man. It should be remembered that many of the immigrants were pleased to make some quick money by substituting. The record includes name of the enrolling man, age, description, for whom substituting, and date of enrollment. The files from this record group are uneven, quality differing from district to district and some have been lost. The Statement of Substitutes are part of Record Group 110 at the National Archives and Records Administration I and are not available by mail request. It is necessary to know the Congressional District where the male was residing.

Case Files on Drafted Aliens

Case Files on Drafted Aliens are files that concern only aliens who were drafted and released from 1861-1864. If an ancestor served in the Civil War, further information can be obtained through the Consolidated Lists, his Military Service Record, or possibly a pension file. The records in the Case Files on Drafted Aliens are part of Record Group 59 which are the general records of the Department of State. The files may include name, district from which drafted, country of citizenship, age, length of time in the United States, and a physical description. The information found in the files varies and may even include a Declaration of Intention for citizenship or similar information. The records are arranged in alphabetical order by surname. The Congressional District is not necessary for access. The records in this group are available by mail requests from National Archives and Record Administration II. It is advised to list the state and county of residence of the person to narrow down the scope of the search.

Mail Requests: Two types of records can be ordered by mail: Consolidated Lists and Case Files of Drafted Aliens.

Congressional Districts: The Congressional District number is necessary when researching the following record groups: Consolidated Lists, Descriptive Rolls, Medical Record of Examinations, and Statement of Substitutes.

Free Transcriptions Available: As of the date of publication, there is no charge for mail requests on any of the records that are available by mail. All of the records at National Archives and Records Administration are held in tightly bound volumes and have not yet been microfilmed. The Archives can provide a *transcription* of the record for free.

Microfilm Copies Available: The information that the archives can send that are free at this time are *transcriptions*. They also provide a service of microfilming the records upon request. This is done for a minimal fee. It should be remembered to give as much identifying information when sending for mail requests such as Name, County of Residence, Age, Marital Status, Congressional District.

Point to Remember: Drafted men comprised 2 1/2% of all those who served the Union in the Civil War. Paid substitutes made up to 5% of those who served, but the draft records can be surveyed for information on ancestors who did not enlist. The main effect of the draft was to fill the ranks of the volunteer units to fight for the Union.

Addresses

Record Group 110
National Archives & Records Administration
700 Pennsylvainia Ave NW
Wahington, DC 20408
Phone: (202) 501-5400

Record Group 59 - State Department
National Archives & Records Administration
Archives II
8601 Adelphi Road
College Park, MD 20740-6001
Phone: (301) 713-7230

See Also

Morebeck, Nancy J. *Civil War Draft Records, An Index to the 38th Congressional Districts of 1863*, Vacaville, CA: Morebeck Publishers, 1997.

Portrait of Pvt. Philip Carper, 35th Battalion, Virginia Cavalry, C.S.A. *Library of Congress, Prints & Photographs Division (LC-B8184-10018)*

3

Confederate Draft Records

Conscription on both sides came about as the result of decreasing numbers of volunteers in the second year of the war. The Confederate States were the first to enact a draft for filling their ranks. Their national conscription act was adopted on 16 April 1862 (1 Cong. C.S.A. Stat. 29). It authorized a call-up of all white men between the ages of 18 and 35 for a 3-year term, bound men already in the Army to serve for three years and allowed units to reorganize and elect their own officers. Later in the year, the age limit was raised to 45 and by 1864, the lower limit was set at 17. In 1864 men between 45 and 50 were conscripted for local defense and detail duty. Also, in 1864, the enrollment of free Negroes and the employment of 20,000 slaves were authorized for auxiliary service.

Originally the administration of conscription activities was under the direction of the Adjutant and Inspector General's Office. A Bureau of Conscription was created on 30 December 1862 through the AIGO General Order 112. The Conscription records are found in RG 109, War Department Collection of Confederate Records. A majority of the records that exist are for the state of Virginia.

If the individual you are researching was in any of the following occupations, there is the possibility of his being granted an exemption:

agriculturist	apothecary
Confederate official	minister
State official	teacher
Railroad employee	mail contractor
physician	newspaper employee
druggist	editor

A person could be detailed in support of the war effort. These persons were: agriculturists, tanners, millers, blacksmiths, shoemakers, wheelwrights, government bureau, artisans and mechanics, contractors to furnish supplies, and telegraph companies. The importance of the railroads to the war effort is shown by exemptions for the following occupations: railroad agents, station agents, baggage masters, conductors, brakemen, carpenters, machinist, fireman, tie contractor, blacksmith, engineers, wood contractor, and pattern maker. Those in civil administration were exempted for the following occupations: judge, justice, magistrate, constable, tax collector, jailer, clerk of court, commissioner, postmaster, sheriff, deputy sheriff, salt agent, legislator, member of the board of police, and probate clerk. The disabled and Overseers were exempt.

In addition to exemptions, the hiring of a paid substitute was also allowed for fees up to $1,000. This practice was eliminated by 1864.

The Records of the Virginia Conscription Office found in the National Archives include:

Commandants' Exemption Books for Virginia 1864-65. 2 vols.

Record of Exemptions in Virginia, 1862-64. 2 vols.

Record of Exemptions for Cause in Virginia, 1864. 1 vol.

Agricultural Exemption Book for Virginia, 1864. 1 vol.

List of Details and Exemptions in Virginia to August 1864. 1 vol.

Register of Applications for Details, Virginia, 1864. 1 vol.

Agricultural Detail Books for Virginia, 1864-65. 2 vols.

Lists of Conscripts from Virginia Recommended for Discharge under General Orders no. 107, 1863. 1 vol.

District of Columbia. Company E, 4th U.S. Colored Infantry, at Fort Lincoln.
Library of Congress, Prints & Photographs Division (LC-B8171-7890)

4

Union Compiled Military Service Records

(CMSR) Microfilm Publications —
National Archives Record Group 94

After finding your ancestor's military unit, more information is available on your ancestor by obtaining the Compiled Military Service Record. Remember this record is only available for Volunteers, not regular Army. There currently is no master index to the names of soldiers who served in the Union volunteer regiments. Individual state indexes are available for all northern and southern states except South Carolina. Remember the indexes are available on microfilm both through the National Archives and the Family History Library. Also, while some of the Compiled Military Service Records are available through the Family History Library, others must be ordered through the National Archives using their photo duplication service and NATF Form 86. This form has replaced the old form NATF Form 80 as of November 2000.

Each volunteer soldier has one Compiled Military Service Record (CMSR) for each regiment in which he served. The records contain basic information about the soldier's military career. The CMSR is an envelope or jacket containing one or more cards. The cards indicate that the soldier was present or absent during a certain period of time. Other cards may indicate date of enlistment and discharge, amount of bounty paid him,

Locating Union and Confederate Records

Harrison. Joseph 152nd Inf. Co.E Sgt.
Harrison, Joseph 170th Inf. Co.F
Harrison, Joseph D. 164th Inf. Co.A
Harrison, Joseph E. 94th Inf. Co.B
Harrison, Joseph G. 152nd Inf. Co.H
Harrison. Kimmel K. 125th Inf. Co.C
Harrison, Lawson C. (L.C.) 11th Inf. Co.D
Harrison, Lawson C. 11th Inf. (3 mo. '61) Co.D
Harrison. Leonard (or Leonard S.) 166th Inf. Co.I Sgt.
Harrison, Lewis 173rd Inf. Co.K
Harrison, Lewis 183rd Inf.
Harrison. Lewis Perry (Lewis P.) 91st Inf. Co.D
Harrison, Lorenzo 9th Cav. Co.I
Harrison, Lorenzo D. 7th Cav. Co.B
Harrison. Lorenzo D. (or Lorenzo) 138th Inf. Co.G
Harrison. Mahlon T. 95th Inf. Co.I
Harrison, Manuel J. 105th Inf. Co.I
Harrison. Martin 11th Cav.
Harrison, Milton J. 86th Inf. (3 mo. '62) Co.B Music.
Harrison, Milton J. 129th Inf. Co.H
Harrison, Moses S. (Moses) 76th Inf. Co.D
Harrison, Orlin 72nd Inf. Co.A
Harrison, Orlin W. (or Orlin) 169th Inf. Co.B Sgt.
Harrison, Pat 1st Inf. (3 mo. '61) Co.G
Harrison, Patterson C. (Patterson) 81st Inf. Co.E
Harrison, Peter 15th Inf.
Harrison, Peter 61st Inf. Co.G
Harrison, Reuben 69th Inf. Co.A
Harrison, Richard 185th Inf.
Harrison, Richard B. 113th Inf. Co.B
Harrison, Richard H. (Richard) 3rd Inf. Co.H
Harrison. Richard L. 2nd Hvy.Arty. Co.H
Harrison, Robert 32nd Inf. Co.H
Harrison, Salathiel 105th Inf. Co.I
Harrison, Samuel 43rd Inf. Co.E
Harrison, Samuel A. 2nd Inf. (3 mo. '61) Co.A
Harrison, Samuel H. 84th Inf. Co.E
Harrison, Samuel H. 124th Inf. Co.H Cpl.
Harrison, Samuel J. 8th Cav. Co.G 2nd Lt.
Harrison, Samuel T. 63rd Inf.
Harrison, Samuel T. 131st Inf. Co.C
Harrison, Sanford 166th Inf. Co.I Cpl.
Harrison, Scott 114th Inf. Co.D Capt.
Harrison, Stephen W. 135th Inf. Co.D
Harrison, Sylvester 177th Inf. Co.G
Harrison, Sylvester 191st Inf.
Harrison, Theodore (Theodore F.) 34th Inf. Co.F
Harrison. Theodore F. 36th Inf. Co.F
Harrison. Thomas Lt.Arty. 22nd Ind.Bty.
Harrison, Thomas 103rd Inf. Co.H
Harrison, William (William H.) 6th Cav. Co.E
Harrison, William 10th Cav. Co.F
Harrison, William 25th Inf. Co.A
Harrison, William 32nd Inf. Co.K
Harrison, William 47th Inf. Co.A,C
Harrison. William 50th Inf. Co.F
Harrison. William (William H.) 60th Inf. (1 yr. '62) Co.F
Harrison. William (or William H.) 83rd Inf. Co.E Music.
Harrison, William 107th Inf. Co.E,D Capt.
Harrison, William 167th Inf. Co.E
Harrison. William C. 97th Inf. Co.I Sgt.

Harrison, William E. 48th Inf. Co.G
Harrison, William G. 124th Inf. Co.E
Harrison, William H. 8th Cav. Co.I
Harrison, William H. 10th Cav. Co.D
Harrison, William H. 1st Hvy.Arty. Co.M
Harrison, William H. 2nd Hvy.Arty. Co.H Sgt.
Harrison, William H. Lt.Arty. 4th Ind.Bty.
Harrison, William H. Lt.Arty. 17th Ind.Bty.
Harrison, William H. 1st Inf. (3 mo. '61) Co.D Cpl.
Harrison, William H. 5th Inf. Co.K Sgt.
Harrison, William H. 8th Inf. (3 mo. '61) Co.G
Harrison, William H. 11th Inf. Co.E
Harrison, William H. 20th Inf. Co.K
Harrison, William H. 42nd Inf. Co.D
Harrison, William H. 45th Inf. Co.B
Harrison, William H. 52nd Inf. Co.B
Harrison, William H. (William) 54th Inf. Co.E
Harrison, William H. 58th Inf. Co.K
Harrison, William H. 98th Inf. Co.D.E
Harrison, William H. 110th Inf. Co.G
Harrison, William H. 122nd Inf. Co.K
Harrison, William H. 128th Inf. Co.C
Harrison, William H. 133rd Inf. Co.H
Harrison, William H. 149th Inf. Co.I Cpl.
Harrison, William H. 171st Inf. Co.A
Harrison, William H. 189th Inf.
Harrison, William H. 192nd Inf. Co.F Cpl.
Harrison, William T. 152nd Inf. Co.H
Harrison, Zachariah 25th Inf. Co.D
Harrison, Zachariah 34th Inf. Co.G
Harrison, Zachariah 189th Inf.
Harriss, Bishop A. 16th Inf. Co.I
Harriss, David W. 120th Inf. Co.K
Harriss, Isaac 102nd Inf. Co.G
Harriss, James M. (James M.C.) 102nd Inf. Co.G
Harriss. Jonathan A. 102nd Inf. Co.D
Harriss, Joseph A. 102nd Inf. Co.G Cpl.
Harriss, Joseph R. 102nd Inf. Co.G Sgt.
Harrisson, William H. 20th Inf. (3 mo. '61) Co.E
Harrit, Richard E. 21st Inf. (3 mo. '61) Co.A
Harritt, Joshua 147th Inf. Co.K
Harritt, Marion 21st Inf. Co.D
Harritt, Richard E. 21st Inf. Co.A Sgt.
Harritt, William 147th Inf. Co.K
Harriyon, James 12th Inf.
Harrmonsderfer, John A. 9th Inf. Co.A
Harrod, Adam 118th Inf. Co.B
Harrod, Barnard Lt.Arty. 4th Ind.Bty.
Harrod, David B. 132nd Inf. Co.C Cpl.
Harrod. Enos 118th Inf. Co.C Sgt.
Harrod, Hamilton 118th Inf. Co.B
Harrod. James (or James B.) 118th Inf. Co.B Cpl.
Harrod. John 132nd Inf. Co.C Sgt.
Harrod, John H. 1st Inf. Co.G
Harrod, John H. 4th Inf. (3 mo. '61) Co.G
Harrod, John H. 132nd Inf. Co.C Capt.
Harrod, John Wesley (or J.W.) 1st Cav. Co.C Sgt.
Harrod. Mills 142nd Inf. Co.C 2nd Lt.
Harrod, Milton S. 45th Inf. Co.D
Harrod, Minor S. 111th Inf. Co.D Sgt.
Harrod, Santford 132nd Inf. Co.C Team.
Harrod, Simon 32nd Inf. Co.F
Harrod. Thomas N. 132nd Inf. Co.C Cpl.
Harrod, William L. 32nd Inf. Co.C 1st Lt.

Harrold, Alfred 74th Inf. Co.C
Harrold, Barnard D. 69th Inf. Co.D
Harrold, Bernardo D. 121st Inf. Co.G
Harrold, William M. (William) 78th Inf. Co.F
Harrold, William W. 115th Inf. Co.E
Harroll, Benjamin S. 146th Inf. Co.F
Harroll, John 7th Cav. Co.C
Harron, Henry O. 187th Inf.
Harrop, Grafton 62nd Inf. Co.A
Harrop, Jacob 50th Inf. Co.B Cpl.
Harrop, Jacob 62nd Inf. Co.A
Harrop, Richard 5th Cav. Co.K
Harrop, Richard 26th Inf. Co.I
Harrop, Rufus H. 97th Inf. Co.K
Harrop, Samuel 91st Inf. Co.B Cpl.
Harrop, Stephen 122nd Inf. Co.I
Harrop, Stephen 178th Inf. Co.F
Harrop, Stephen 185th Inf.
Harroun. Alexander D. 29th Inf. Co.F
Harroun, Andrew J. 29th Inf. Co.F
Harroun, Henry E. (or Henry) 128th Inf. Co.G
Harrow, James 16th Inf. (3 mo. '61) Co.K
Harrow, John 173rd Inf.
Harruff, Henry 174th Inf. Co.K
Harruff, Henry 180th Inf.
Harruff, James 50th Inf. Co.F
Harruff, James 99th Inf. Co.B
Harruff, James P. 174th Inf. Co.K
Harruff, James P. 180th Inf.
Harruff, William 50th Inf. Co.F .
Harruff, William 99th Inf. Co.B
Harry 57th Inf. Co.K
Harry, Abraham P. (Abraham) 65th Inf. Co.E
Harry, Albert J. 184th Inf. Co.B,C
Harry, Albert J. 188th Inf.
Harry, Augustus 102nd Inf. Co.F
Harry, Benjamin F. 1st Hvy.Any. Co.I
Harry, Benjamin F. (Benjamin) 89th Inf. Co.C
Harry, Charles A. 169th Inf. Co.E
Harry, Daniel 1st Hvy.Arty. Co.A
Harry, Edwin 153rd Inf. Co.G.H
Harry, Henry 1st Inf. (3 mo. '61) Co.F
Harry, Henry 73rd Inf. Co.F
Harry, James M. 162nd Inf. Co.B
Harry, Joseph H. 12th Cav. Co.K Saddler
Harry, Permanio 73rd Inf. Co.B
Harry, Robert 60th Inf. (1 yr. '62) Co.D Capt.
Harry, Samuel M. 63rd Inf. Co.I
Harry, Samuel M. 112th Inf. Colliflower's Co.
Harry, Silas C. 104th Inf. Co.K
Harry, William 12th Cav. Co.K
Harry, William 40th Inf. Co.K
Harry, William 93rd Inf. Co.E
Harry, William 179th Inf. Co.E
Harry, William 183rd Inf.
Harry, William H. 12th Cav. (3 mo. '61) Co.E Sgt.
Harry, William H. 110th Inf. Co.D,E Adj.
Harryman. Harrison 62nd Inf. Co.B
Harsberger, Jonas 20th Inf. Co.B Cpl.
Harsch, Thomas J. 191st Inf. Co.A
Harsel, Andrew I. (or J.) 9th Cav. Co.H
Harsen, Benjamin 25th Inf. Co.C
Harsh, Abel 126th Inf. Co.F
Harsh, Abraham 151st Inf. Co.A
Harsh, Asbury 126th Inf. Co.F Cpl.
Harsh, Benjamin 157th Inf. Co.K

Janet B. Hewett, editor, The Roster of Union Soldiers, 1861-1865, Ohio. *Wilmington, NC: Broadfoot Publishing Company, 1998.*

age, residence at the time of enlistment, occupation, a physical description, and information such as wounds received or hospitalization. The place of birth may be indicated. The packet may include personal papers of various kinds including the soldier's enlistment papers, any papers relating to his capture or release, etc. The CMSR records were created by the War Department after the war as a more rapid and efficient means of checking military and medical records in connection with claims for pensions and other veteran's benefits.

New Book - Best Ever

The fastest way to find the military unit in which your soldier served is by using the new publication of volumes called *The Roster of Union Soldiers* which has copied soldier's name and the unit he served in from the entries of the National Archives' Union Compiled Military Service Records. This publication helps one rapidly find the unit in which the soldier served. One must first know the state under which the soldier volunteered, however, as the records are compiled by state. This book gives the name of the *unit* in which your ancestor served.

Hewett, Janet B., editor. *The Roster of Union Soldiers.* Wilmington, NC: Broadfoot Publishing Company, 1998. 33 Volumes.

To find specific microfilm numbers for indexes with the Family History Library Catalog, search under locality section under [STATE] - MILITARY RECORDS - CIVIL WAR, 1861-1865 - INDEXES. For service records, search the Locality section under [STATE] - MILITARY RECORDS - CIVIL WAR, 1861-1865 or use the table beginning on the next page.

STATE	NATIONAL ARCHIVES # *	FHL MICROFILM #
Alabama Index	M263	880848
Alabama CMSR	M276	1276618 - 1276620
Arizona Index	M532	881608
Arkansas Index	M383	881488 - 881491
Arkansas CMSR	M399	1380796 - 1380855
California Index	M533	881609 - 881615
Colorado Index	M534	821998 - 822000
Connecticut Index	M535	821909 - 821925
Dakota Index	M536	881616
Delaware Index	M537	881617 - 881620
DC Index	M538	881964 - 881966
Florida Index	M264	821767
Florida CMSR	M400	1299987 - 1299997
Georgia Index	M385	881394
Georgia CMSR	M403	1276608
Illinois Index	M539	881621 - 881721
Indiana Index	M540	881722 - 881807
Iowa Index	M541	881808 - 881836
Kansas Index	M542	881837 - 881846
Kentucky Index	M386	881492 - 881521
Kentucky CMSR	M397	1487066 - 1487275
		1489753 - 1490057
Louisiana Index	M387	821926 - 821929
Louisiana CMSR	M396	1380930 - 1380979
Maine Index	M543	881847 - 881869
Maryland Index	M388	881522 - 881534
Maryland CMSR	M384	1477976 -1478213
Massachusetts Index	M544	881870 - 881913
Michigan Index	M545	881914 - 881961
Minnesota Index	M546	821930 - 821938
		882902
Mississippi Index	M389	881535
Mississippi CMSR	M404	1292659 - 1292662
Missouri Index	M390	881536 - 881589

Missouri CMSR	M405	1500223 - 1501075
Nebraska Index	M547	821905 - 821906
Nevada Index	M548	821939
New Jersey Index	M550	882031 - 882056
New Mexico Index	M242	821883 - 821886
New Mexico CMSR	M427	471538 - 471583
New York Index	M551	882057 - 882213
North Carolina Index	M391	881590 - 881591
North Carolina CMSR	M401	1473248 - 1473272
Ohio Index	M552	882214 - 882335
Oregon Index	M553	821947
Pennsylvania Index	M554	882336 - 882471
Rhode Island Index	M555	821940 - 821946
Tennessee Index	M392	821889 - 821904
Tennessee CMSR	M395	1482042 - 1482261
Texas Index	M393	881592 - 881593
Texas CMSR	M402	1292646 - 1292658
Utah Index	M556	1292645
Utah CMSR	M692	821588
Vermont Index	M557	882472 - 882485
Virginia Index	M394	881594
Virginia CMSR	M398	1292638 - 1292644
Washington Index	M558	821948
West Virginia Index	M507	881595 - 881607
West Virginia CMSR	M508	1478231 - 1478475
		1482026 - 1482041
Wisconsin Index	M559	882486 - 882518
Veteran Reserve Corps. Index	M636	1205358 - 1205383
Colored Troops Index	M589	1266617 - 1266643
		1266546 - 1266616
Not raised by States Index	M1290	1604884 - 1604920
Former Confederates Galvanized Yankees (former POW's)	M1017	1315687 - 1315751

*HeritageQuest films for most states are available for purchase or rent. See chapter 22.

Locating Union and Confederate Records

Samuel Harrop, compiled military service record
(Corporal, 91st Ohio Infantry, Co. B.) *Washington, D.C.: National Archives.*

Service Records of Sailors

The National Archives has weekly returns of enlistments, 1855 to 1891 that are the most valuable records for sailors. They have not been filmed and are available only at the National Archives in Record Group 24, Records of the Bureau of Naval Personnel. Entries list the sailor's name, enlistment date, birthplace, age, occupation, personal description, date of or return of enlistment, and records of previous naval service.

Index to Rendezvous Reports, Civil War, 1861-1865. An alphabetical surname index to sailors who enlisted by National Archives Microfilm Publication is available both at the National Archives and the Family History Library.

STATE	NATIONAL ARCHIVES #	FHL MICROFILM #
All	T1099	1570558 - 1570588

Records of Naval Officers

Powell, William H. editor. *Officers of the Army and Navy (Volunteer) Who Served in the Civil War.* Philadelphia, PA: L.R. Hamersly & Co., 1893.

Powell, William H. editor. *Officers of the Army and Navy (Regular) Who Served in the Civil War.* Philadelphia, PA: L.R. Hamersly & Co., 1892.

Union—Galvanized Yankees

The soldiers of the 1st through 6th U.S. Volunteer Infantry regiment, 1864-1866, were Confederate prisoners of war who gained their release from prison by enlisting in the Union Army. The service records have been compiled and are alphabetically listed under the regiment in which they served. The units were assigned to areas where they would not have to fight their former comrades, the West. The soldiers protected the settlers from Indians, restored stage and mail service, guarded survey parties for the Union Pacific Railroad, escorted supply trains, and rebuilt telegraph lines.

There are two indexes to this set of records available through the National Archives. Neither is complete. One index list the names of all the soldiers who served in U.S. Volunteer Infantry units. The index states the following:

> Name
>
> Rank
>
> Unit in which served

The other is an alphabetical list of the names of Confederate POW's who enlisted in U.S. service. The index states the following:

> Name
>
> Confederate rank and regiment

Sometimes the records also list the following:

> Union regiment
>
> When and where captured
>
> When and where mustered into Union Service
>
> Date of release from prison
>
> Date of oath of allegiance

The indexes are available at the National Archives in Film group M1017. Neither index is available through the Family History Center.

Compiled Service Records of Former Confederate Soldiers Who Served in the 1st through the 6th U.S. Volunteer Infantry Regiments, 1864-1866 (M1017)

The microfilms of the Compiled Service Records of Former Confederate Soldiers Who Served in the 1st through the 6th U.S. Volunteer

Infantry Regiments, 1864-1866 are available through the National Archives and the Family History Library.

UNIT	NATIONAL ARCHIVES M1017	FHL MICROFILM #
1st U.S. Volunteers	M 1017 rolls 1-14	1315687 - 1315700
2nd U.S. Volunteers	M 1017 rolls 15-24	1315701 - 1315710
3rd U.S. Volunteers	M 1017 rolls 25-33	1315711 - 1315719
4th U.S. Volunteers	M 1017 rolls 34-39	1315720 - 1315725
5th U.S. Volunteers	M 1017 rolls 40-52	1315726 - 1315738
6th U.S. Volunteers	M 1017 rolls 53-64	1315739 - 1315750
Personal papers	M 1017 roll 65	1315751

Copies are also available through the National Archives using their photo duplication service and NATF Form 86. NATF Form 80 has been replaced by NATF Forms 85 and 86. (See the National Archives Reproduction Services chapter).

Charleston, S.C. Battery of Confederate Fort Johnson; Fort Sumter in distance. *1865. Library of Congress, Prints & Photographs Division (LC-B8171-3064)*

5

Confederate Compiled Military Service Records

(CMSR) Microfilm Publications — National Archives Record Group 109

Some of the military records of the Confederate Government were passed into the hands of the Union Army's officers in the final days of the war. These were sent to the War Department in Washington, DC. After the war, the War Department was loaned, by most southern states, their Confederate military personnel records for copying. These captured and copied Confederate records, as well as Union prison and parole records, were abstracted by the War department to compile military service records of Confederate officers, noncommissioned offices, and enlisted men. Each man's service record consists of a jacket or envelope which gives his name, his rank at entry into service and exit from service, and the unit in which he served, and often a statement concerning the origin or background of that unit. Cross references at the bottom of the jacket sometimes mention other units to which the soldier belonged. Within the jacket are such things as card extracts from pay musters, hospital records, prisoner-of-war registers, parole ledgers, general or special orders from army headquarters, appointment books, and promotion lists. Many service records include no original manuscripts—just the card extracts.

Duff, J.M. VA 64th Mtd.Inf. Co.B
Duff, Joel KY 2nd Bn.Mtd.Rifles Co.D
Duff, John AR Inf. Ballard's Co.
Duff, John MO 6th Inf. Co.K
Duff, John TN 62nd Mtd.Inf. Co.E
Duff, John TX 23rd Cav. Co.H
Duff, John TX 23rd Cav. Co.K
Duff, John A. AL Lt.Arty. 2nd Bn. Co.C Cpl.
Duff, John A. VA 6th Bn.Res. Co.F
Duff, John E. LA 31st Inf. Co.B Cpl.
Duff, John F. TX Cav. Mann's Regt. Co.A
Duff, John F. TX Cav. Mann's Bn. Co.A
Duff, John G. VA 37th Inf. Co.B
Duff, John G. VA 37th Inf. Co.B
Duff, John H. MS 23rd Inf. Co.I
Duff, John J. NC 3rd Inf. Co.B
Duff, John L. MS 2nd Inf. Co.G
Duff, John R. MS 33rd Inf. Co.K
Duff, John R. TN 36th Inf. Co.E
Duff, John S.B. VA 37th Inf. Co.B
Duff, John V. VA 37th Inf. Co.C Capt.
Duff, Joseph SC 5th St.Troops Co.K
Duff, Joseph TN 2nd (Ashby's) Cav. Co.G
Duff, Joseph TN 37th Inf. Co.G
Duff, J.P. MS 10th Cav. Co.A 1st Lt.
Duff, J.R. MS 3rd Inf. Co.K
Duff, J.R. MS 22nd Inf. Co.F
Duff, J.T. AR 38th Inf. New Co.I
Duff, J.T. NC 30th Inf. Co.E
Duff, J.W. TX 11th Cav. Co.I Cpl.
Duff, Lawrence AL Inf. 2nd Regt. Co.F
Duff, Lawrence LA Pointe Coupee Arty.
Duff, Lawrence C. Conf.Inf. 1st Bn. Co.I 2nd Lt.
Duff, M. GA 4th (Clinch's) Cav. Co.H
Duff, Madison F. VA 6th Bn.Res. Co.F Sgt.
Duff, Marcus KY 13th Cav. Co.G
Duff, Marion J. TX 2nd Cav. Co.K Sgt.
Duff, M.B. MS 23rd Inf. Co.I
Duff, Michael AL 8th Inf. Co.I
Duff, Michael H. VA 37th Inf. Co.F 2nd Lt.
Duff, Nathaniel H. VA 37th Inf. Co.H
Duff, Oscar C. VA 37th Inf. Co.C Sgt.
Duff, Parker MS 44th Inf. Co.K
Duff, P.H. AR 1st (Dobbin's) Cav. Co.K
Duff, Preston H. VA 51st Inf. Co.G
Duff, R.A. VA 4th Cav. Co.I
Duff, R.B. VA 16th Cav. Co.A
Duff, Reese B. VA Cav. Ferguson's Bn. Stevenson's Co.
Duff, Reese B. VA 37th Inf. Co.C
Duff, Richard H. VA 55th Inf. Co.A,D Sgt.
Duff, Robert AR 15th (Josey's) Inf. Co.D,E
Duff, Robert TN 35th Inf. 2nd Co.A
Duff, Robert VA 7th Inf. Co.F
Duff, Robert G. VA 37th Inf. Co.H
Duff, Robert J. MS 43rd Inf. Co.E Sgt.
Duff, Rose (Mrs.) SC 1st (Orr's) Rifles Cook,Laundress
Duff, Rufus TN Lt.Arty. Kain's Co.
Duff, Rufus K. TN 34th Inf. Co.F
Duff, Samuel A. 37th Inf. Co.C Cpl.
Duff, Samuel G. VA 37th Inf. Co.K Cpl.
Duff, Samuel H. VA 64th Mtd.Inf. Co.F
Duff, Samuel J. VA 37th Inf. Co.H
Duff, Sanford B. VA Lt.Arty. Pegram's Co.
Duff, Sanford B. VA 57th Inf. Co.H

Duff, Shadrack KY 13th Cav. Co.A
Duff, Thomas AL 7th Inf. Co.D
Duff, Thomas AR 1st (Monroe's) Cav. Co.C
Duff, Thomas AR 11th Inf. Co.E
Duff, Thomas H. TN 37th Inf. Co.G
Duff, Thomas J. VA 50th Inf. Cav.Co.B
Duff, Van B. VA 25th Cav. Co.I,H
Duff, W.A. MS 23rd Inf. Co.I Sgt.
Duff, Walker LA 1st Cav. Co.H
Duff, Walter R. MS 43rd Inf. Co.E
Duff, W.B. TN 5th Inf. 2nd Co.D Cpl.
Duff, W.F. LA Mil.Cont.Regt. Mitchell's Co.
Duff, W.H. LA 25th Inf. Co.I
Duff, W.H. TN Cav. 1st Bn. (McNairy's) Co.C Bugler
Duff, W.H.H. MO Cav. 1st Regt.St.Guard Co.F
Duff, W.H.H. MO 7th Cav. Co.H
Duff, W.H.H. MO 8th Cav. Co.G
Duff, W.H.H. TN Conscr.
Duff, William GA 34th Inf. Co.B
Duff, William VA 64th Mtd.Inf. Co.G
Duff, William F. VA 37th Inf. Co.H Capt.
Duff, William H. TN 32nd Inf. Co.D Ch.Music.
Duff, William J. VA 7th Cav. Co.B 2nd Lt.
Duff, William J. VA 55th Inf. Co.D 1st Lt.
Duff, William L. MS 17th Inf. Co.K Maj.
Duff, William L. TX 9th (Young's) Inf. Co.D
Duff, William M. TX 34th Cav. Co.C
Duff, William M. VA Hvy.Arty. 19th Bn. Co.D
Duff, William P. VA 50th Inf. Co.G Capt.
Duff, William T. GA 3rd Cav.
Duff, Wm. T. MS 1st Cav. Co.E 2nd Lt.
Duff, William W. MO Cav. 1st Regt.St.Guard Co.F Cpl.
Duff, Wilson A. MS 43rd Inf. Co.E Sgt.
Duff, W.L. MS 8th Cav. Lt.Col.
Duff, W.R. MS 2nd St.Cav. Co.E
Duff, W.R. MS 23rd Inf. Co.I
Duff, W.T. TN 21st Inf. Co.C
Duff, W.T. 9th Conf.Inf. Co.H
Duff, W.W. MO 7th Cav. Co.H Sgt.
Duff, W.W. MO 8th Cav. Co.G Sgt.
Duffan, Henry MD Arty. 3rd Btty.
Duffan, J. LA 9th Inf. Co.C
Duffard, Dominique LA 30th Inf. Co.E
Duffard, Theophile LA Cav. Webb's Co.
Duffart, J. LA Mil. Jackson Rifle Bn.
Duffau, Joseph LA Mil. 1st Native Guards
Duffburrow, H.M. 2nd Conf.Eng.Troops Co.C Sgt.
Duffee, A.C. AL 5th Inf. New Co.G
Duffee, Charles VA 9th Inf. Co.G
Duffee, Cornelius FL Milton Lt.Arty. Dunham's Co.
Duffee, Daniel LA 2nd Inf. Co.G Cpl.
Duffee, H.A. TN 47th Inf. Co.F
Duffee, James GA 25th Inf. Co.A
Duffee, James C. AL 34th Inf. Co.G
Duffee, James H. GA 41st Inf. Co.I
Duffee, James K. AL 19th Inf. Co.K
Duffee, James M. AL Lt.Arty. Hurt's Btty.
Duffee, James W. GA 2nd Cav. Co.E
Duffee, J.L. AL 5th Inf. Co.G
Duffee, John F. AL 34th Inf. Co.G
Duffee, John L. GA 46th Inf. Co.C Cpl.
Duffee, Marion W. MS 1st (Patton's) Inf. Co.C
Duffee, Michael TX 10th Inf. Co.F

Duffee, M.W. MS 37th Inf. Co.H Sgt.
Duffee, Philip LA 6th Inf. Co.H
Duffee, Philip VA Lt.Arty. 13th Bn. Co.B
Duffee, T.G. TN 47th Inf. Co.F
Duffee, Thomas GA 2nd Cav. Co.E
Duffee, T.L. GA 13th Inf. Co.F
Duffee, Willey GA 4th Inf. Co.D Cpl.
Duffee, William MS Lt.Arty. (Brookhaven Lt.Arty.) Hoskins' Btty. Sgt.
Duffee, William H. TN 5th Inf.
Duffee, W.S. AL 1st Cav. 2nd Co.B
Duffee, W.S. GA Inf. (Loc.Def.) Whiteside's Nav.Bn. Co.A
Duffel, Andrew C. AR 5th Inf. Co.G
Duffel, E.N. AR 5th Inf. Co.D,E
Duffel, F.M. LA 2nd Cav. Co.G Cpl.
Duffel, Frederick LA 8th Inf. Co.K 1st Lt.
Duffel, Henry LA Arty. Landry's Co. (Donaldsonville Arty.)
Duffel, Isaac TX 28th Cav. Co.F Bugler
Duffel, James GA 3rd Cav. (St.Guards) Co.G
Duffel, James LA 2nd Cav. Co.G
Duffel, James T. LA 31st Inf. Co.K
Duffel, J.H. AR 5th Inf. Co.D
Duffel, Joel S. GA 51st Inf. Co.I Sgt.
Duffel, John E. LA 8th Inf. Co.K Asst.Surg.
Duffel, Jno. E. Gen. & Staff Asst.Surg.
Duffel, L. LA Mil. Orleans Guards Regt. Co.A
Duffel, Leonse LA 8th Inf. Co.K
Duffel, Martin V.B. LA 8th Inf. Co.I
Duffel, Samuel GA 32nd Inf. Co.F
Duffel, W.H. LA Inf.Cons.Crescent Regt. Co.I Cpl.
Duffel, William A. TN 24th Bn.S.S. Co.A
Duffell, Edward J. GA 36th (Villepigue's) Inf. Co.B
Duffell, Edward J. VA Lt.Arty. 13th Bn. Co.C Sgt.
Duffell, H. Conf.Lt.Arty. Richardson's Bn. Co.B
Duffell, I.H. MO 8th Cav. Co.H
Duffell, J.H. MO 7th Cav. Co.K
Duffell, Newton J. LA 9th Inf. Co.B
Duffell, T.T. AR 30th Inf. Co.L,A,F
Duffell, W.A. KY 2nd (Woodward's) Cav. Co.G
Duffell, William C. GA Arty. 9th Bn. Co.C Cpl.
Duffell, William O. GA 13th Inf. Co.F
Duffels, Charles Conf.Inf. Tucker's Regt. Co.I
Duffer, A.T. TN 20th Inf. Co.F Ord.Sgt.
Duffer, A.T. TN 9th (Ward's) Cav. Co.E
Duffer, Benjamin W. MO 1st N.E. Cav. Co.H
Duffer, Charles H. VA 44th Inf. Co.I
Duffer, J.A. TN 9th (Ward's) Cav. Co.E
Duffer, James E. VA 44th Inf. Co.I
Duffer, James H. VA Arty. Paris' Co.
Duffer, J.E. TN 55th (Brown's) Inf. Co.D
Duffer, John TN 55th (Brown's) Inf. Co.D
Duffer, John VA Inf. 44th Bn. Co.C
Duffer, John H. TN 2nd (Robison's) Inf. Co.I
Duffer, Joseph TN 18th Inf. Co.C
Duffer, M.V. TN 51st Inf. Co.H
Duffer, M.V. TN 51st (Cons.) Inf. Co.D
Duffer, Richard T. VA 44th Inf. Co.I Cpl.
Duffer, R.O. TN 18th Inf. Co.C
Duffer, Robert A. TN Cav. 7th Bn. (Bennett's) Co.A Trump.
Duffer, Robert S. TN Cav. 2nd Bn. (Biffle's) Co.F Cpl.

Hewett, Janet B., Editor. The Roster of Confederate Soldiers 1861-1865. Vol. V. Wilmington, NC: Broadfoot Publishing Company, 1996.

New Book - Best Ever

The fastest way to find the military unit the soldier served in is by using the new publication of volumes which has copied the entries of names and units found in the National Archives' Confederate Compiled Military Service Records. *The Roster of Confederate Soldiers 1861-1865,* edited by Janet B. Hewett in 16 volumes published in Wilmington, NC, by Broadfoot Publishing Company, 1996, is a 16 volume set of a consolidated index to all states' Confederate soldiers. It gives the name and military unit in which the soldier served. It is available in Salt Lake at the Family History Library and at other large archives and libraries. This is the easiest way to find the unit in which your Confederate soldier was enrolled.

Compiled Service Records for Confederate soldiers and officers are available through the National Archives and the Family History Library. For the National Archives film numbers see *Military Service Records: A Select Catalog of National Archives Microfilm Publications* by the National Archives Trust Fund Board, National Archives and Records Administration. Copies are also available through the National Archives using their photo duplication service and NATF Form 86. The previously used NATF Form 80 has been replaced by NATF Forms 85 and 86. (See the National Archives Reproduction Services chapter).

CONFEDERATE COMPILED MILITARY SERVICE RECORDS*

STATE	NATIONAL ARCHIVES #	FHL MICROFILM #
Master Index—All States	M253	191127 - 191661
Alabama Index	M374	821949 - 821997
Alabama CMSR	M311	880330 - 880837
Arizona Index	M375	821837
Arizona CMSR	M318	536241
Arkansas Index	M376	821811 - 821836
Arkansas CMSR	M317	880849 - 881104
Florida Index	M225	880001 - 880009
Florida CMSR	M251	880103 - 880206

Georgia Index	M226	821700 - 821766
Georgia CMSR	M266	1499064 - 1499670
Kentucky Index	M377	881380 - 881393
Kentucky CMSR	M319	1447468 - 1447603
Louisiana Index	M378	881457 - 881487
Louisiana CMSR	M320	1447604 - 1473247
Maryland CMSR	M321	1292663 - 1292683
Mississippi Index	M232	821838 - 821882
Mississippi CMSR	M269	1488026 - 1488452
Missouri Index	M380	882002 - 882017
Missouri CMSR	M322	1500030 - 1500222
North Carolina Index	M230	821768 - 821810
North Carolina CMSR	M270	1381001 - 1381500
		1447001 - 1447080
South Carolina Index	M381	881967 - 882001
South Carolina CMSR	M267	1380691 - 1380695
		1447081 - 1447467
Tennessee Index	M231	880055 - 880102
Tennessee CMSR	M268	1499671 - 1500028
		1427065
Texas Index	M227	880014 - 880054
Texas CMSR	M323	1501077 - 1501521
Virginia Index	M382	881395 - 881456
Virginia CMSR	M324	1488678 - 1489752
		1488739
Directly by Confed. Gov Index	M818	1206310 - 1206335
Directly by Confed. Gov CMSR	M258	880207 - 880329
General & Staff Officers Index	M818	1206310 - 1206335
General & Staff Officers CMSR	M331	881105 - 881379
Unfiled Papers & Slips	M347	1402001 - 1402442

*HeritageQuest films for these records are available for purchase or rent. See chapter 22.

Service of Sailors

RECORDS RELATING TO CONFEDERATE
NAVAL AND MARINE PERSONNEL*

STATE	NATIONAL ARCHIVES #	FHL MICROFILM #
All	M260	191662 - 191668

*To order HeritageQuest films in Series M260 see chapter 22.

Duff, Marcus

Co. G, 13 Kentucky Cavalry

(Confederate.)

Private Private

CARD NUMBERS.

1	4645	20
2	4966	21
3		22
4		23
5		24
6		25
7		26
8		27
9		28
10		29
11		30
12		31
13		32
14		33
15		34
16		35
17		36
18		37
19		38

Number of medical cards herein   0

Number of personal papers herein   0

BOOK MARK:

See also

Marcus Duff, Compiled Military Service Records, Co. G, 13th Kentucky Cavalry.
Washington: National Archives.

Confederate Compiled Military Service Records

(CONFEDERATE.)		
B	13 Cav	Ky

Marcus Duff.

Pvt. Co.G, 10 Regt Ky Mtd Rifles

Appears on a

RECEIPT ROLL

for clothing,

for _____2 Qr_____ , 186 4 .

Date of issue: Apr 7 , 186 4 .
Signature ....
Remarks:

Roll No. ....

Chenault.

Copyist.

(Confederate.)		
S	13 Cav.	Ky.

Mc Duff

Pvt | Capt. H. M. Combs' Company of Kentucky Infantry.*

Appears on a

Muster Roll

of the organization named above mustered into service October 14, 1862,

for _____Mel. dated_____ , 186 .

Age ....
Residence _____Breathitt_____
Enlisted:
When _____Oct. 1_____ , 186 2.
Where _____Breathitt_____
By whom _____N. Z. Caudill_____
Period ....

Present or absent _____Not Stated_____
Remarks:

*This company subsequently became Company G, 13th Regiment Kentucky Cavalry.
The regiment was known at various times as Caudill's Regiment Kentucky Infantry, 10th Regiment Kentucky Infantry, 10th Regiment Kentucky Mounted Riflemen, and 11th Regiment Kentucky Mounted Infantry. The 11th Regiment Kentucky Mounted Infantry became the 13th Regiment Kentucky Cavalry by S. O. No. 44, A. & I. G. O. dated February 22, 1865.

Book mark : ....

(650) M. Shearin
Copyist.

(Confederate.)		
S	13 Cav.	Ky.

Marcus Duff

Pvt , Co. G, 10 Reg't Kentucky Infantry.*

Appears on

Company Muster Roll

of the organization named above,

for _____Enlistment to Dec't_____ , 186 2.

Enlisted:
When _____Oct. 1_____ , 186 .
Where _____Breathet Cty_____
By whom _____Capt. Combs_____
Period _____3 yrs_____

Last paid:
By whom _____never paid_____
To what time .... , 186 .

Present or absent _____Present_____
Remarks: ....

*This company subsequently became Company G, 13th Regiment Kentucky Cavalry.
The regiment was known at various times as Caudill's Regiment Kentucky Infantry, 10th Regiment Kentucky Infantry, 10th Regiment Kentucky Mounted Riflemen, and 11th Regiment Kentucky Mounted Infantry. The 11th Regiment Kentucky Mounted Infantry became the 13th Regiment Kentucky Cavalry by S. O. No. 44, A. & I. G. O. dated February 22, 1865.

Book mark : ....

(642) M. Shearin
Copyist.

(Confederate.)		
S	13 Cav.	Ky.

Markus Duff

Pvt , Co. G, Caudill's Reg't, Kentucky Infantry.*

Appears on

Company Muster Roll

of the organization named above,

for _____Dec 31st 1862 to Ap't 30_____ , 186 3.

Enlisted:
When _____Oct. 1_____ , 186 .
Where _____Breathitt_____
By whom _____Col. Caudill_____
Period _____3 yr._____

Last paid:
By whom _____Maj. Crutchfield_____
To what time _____Dec. 31_____ , 186 .

Present or absent _____Present_____
Remarks: ....

*This company subsequently became Company G, 13th Regiment Kentucky Cavalry.
The regiment was known at various times as Caudill's Regiment Kentucky Infantry, 10th Regiment Kentucky Infantry, 10th Regiment Kentucky Mounted Riflemen, and 11th Regiment Kentucky Mounted Infantry. The 11th Regiment Kentucky Mounted Infantry became the 13th Regiment Kentucky Cavalry by S. O. No. 44, A. & I. G. O. dated February 22, 1865.

Book mark : ....

(642) M. Shearin
Copyist.

(Confederate.)		
S	13 Cav.	Ky.

Marcus Duff

Pvt , Co. G, 10 Reg't Kentucky Infantry.*

Appears on

Company Muster Roll

of the organization named above,

for _____Ap'l 30 to Aug 31_____ , 186 3.

Enlisted:
When _____Oct. 1_____ , 186 1.
Where _____Whitesburg_____
By whom _____Col. Caudill_____
Period _____3_____

Last paid:
By whom _____Maj. Crutchfield_____
To what time _____Ap'l 31_____ , 186 .

Present or absent _____Present_____
Remarks: ....

*This company subsequently became Company G, 13th Regiment Kentucky Cavalry.
The regiment was known at various times as Caudill's Regiment Kentucky Infantry, 10th Regiment Kentucky Infantry, 10th Regiment Kentucky Mounted Riflemen, and 11th Regiment Kentucky Mounted Infantry. The 11th Regiment Kentucky Mounted Infantry became the 13th Regiment Kentucky Cavalry by S. O. No. 44, A. & I. G. O. dated February 22, 1865.

Book mark : ....

(642) M. Shearin
Copyist.

(Confederate.)		
S	13 Cav.	Ky.

Marcus Duff

Pvt , Co. G, 10 Regiment Kentucky Mounted Riflemen.*

Appears on

Company Muster Roll

of the organization named above,

for _____Aug 31 to Dec 31_____ , 186 3.

Enlisted:
When _____Sep't 26_____ , 186 2.
Where _____Perry County_____
By whom _____Col. Caudill_____
Period _____3 yr._____

Last paid:
By whom _____Crutchfield_____
To what time _____Aug 31_____ , 186 .

Present or absent _____Present_____
Remarks: ....

*This company subsequently became Company G, 13th Regiment Kentucky Cavalry.
The regiment was known at various times as Caudill's Regiment Kentucky Infantry, 10th Regiment Kentucky Infantry, 10th Regiment Kentucky Mounted Riflemen, and 11th Regiment Kentucky Mounted Infantry. The 11th Regiment Kentucky Mounted Infantry became the 13th Regiment Kentucky Cavalry by S. O. No. 44, A. & I. G. O. dated February 22, 1865.

Book mark : ....

(642) M. Shearin
Copyist.

Marcus Duff, Compiled Military Service Records, Co. G, 13th Kentucky Cavalry.
Washington: National Archives.

Westover Landing, Va. Lt. Col. Samuel W. Owens, 3d Pennsylvania Cavalry, caught napping. *Alexander Gardner, 1862 August. Library of Congress, Prints & Photographs Division (LC-B8171-0625)*

6

National Archives Reproduction Schedules

In November of 2000, the National Archives and Records Administration (NARA) revamped to the system and fees for providing copies of the Military Service Records (Compiled Military Service Records) and Pension Application Files. The NATF Form 80 which was used previously for both the Service Records and the Pension Records has been discontinued. NATF Form 85 is now used for Pension Files and Form 86 for Military Service Records. There is a proposed change in the fee schedule also. To request the Form NATF Form 85 or NATF Form 86 send an email to *inquire@nara.gov* or by mail to request the forms: General Reference Branch (NNRG-P), National Archives and Records Administration, 7th and Pennsylvania Ave. NW, Washington, DC 20408. You can request several forms per request. State your mailing address, which form needed as well as number of forms needed. The NATF Form 85 for Pensions is the same form used for Bounty Land Warrants. *No Bounty Land Warrants were issued for Civil War Service.* Bounty Lands were used for military service prior to 1855. Note also that with the Union Pension you may request Full Pension Application File for a fee of $37.00 or the Pension Documents Packet for a fee of $14.75.

Locating Union and Confederate Records

NATIONAL ARCHIVES TRUST FUND BOARD   NATF Form 85 (9-2000)

OMB Control No. 3095-0032 Expires 12-31-2001

F112066 — NATIONAL ARCHIVES ORDER FOR COPIES OF FEDERAL PENSION OR BOUNTY LAND WARRANT APPLICATIONS (See Instructions page before completing this form)

SECTION A. 1. INDICATE BELOW THE TYPE OF FILE TO BE SEARCHED (Check ONE box only)

If we locate the file you identify below, we will make copies as indicated. There is no charge for an unsuccessful search.

☐ **Full Pension Application File:** The cost for copies is $37.

☐ **Pension Documents Packet:** (See instructions.) The cost for copies is $14.75.

☐ **Bounty-Land Warrant Application:** The cost for copies is $17.25.

REQUIRED MINIMUM IDENTIFICATION OF VETERAN - MUST BE COMPLETED OR YOUR ORDER CANNOT BE SERVICED

2. VETERAN (Give last, first, and middle names)

3. BRANCH OF SERVICE IN WHICH HE SERVED ☐ ARMY ☐ NAVY ☐ MARINE CORPS

4. STATE FROM WHICH HE SERVED

5. WAR IN WHICH, OR DATES BETWEEN WHICH, HE SERVED

◆ If service was Civil War, UNION SERVICE ONLY. See reverse of Instructions page.

PLEASE PROVIDE THE FOLLOWING ADDITIONAL INFORMATION, IF KNOWN

6. UNIT IN WHICH HE SERVED (Name of regiment or number, company, etc., name of ship)

7. IF SERVICE WAS ARMY, ARM IN WHICH HE SERVED ☐ INFANTRY ☐ CAVALRY ☐ ARTILLERY   If other, specify:

8. Rank ☐ OFFICER ☐ ENLISTED

9. KIND OF SERVICE ☐ VOLUNTEER ☐ REGULARS

10. PENSION/BOUNTY-LAND FILE NO.

11. IF VETERAN LIVED IN A HOME FOR SOLDIERS, GIVE LOCATION (City and State)

12. PLACE(S) VETERAN LIVED AFTER SERVICE

13. DATE OF BIRTH

14. PLACE OF BIRTH (City, County, State, etc.)

17. NAME OF WIDOW OR OTHER CLAIMANT

15. DATE OF DEATH

16. PLACE OF DEATH (City, County, State, etc.)

SECTION B. THIS SPACE IS FOR OUR REPLY TO YOU. PLEASE GO TO SECTION C.

We were unable to search for the file you requested above. No payment is required. Your request is returned because:

☐ BLOCK 1 IS NOT CHECKED and we are unable to determine which type of file you are requesting.

☐ MORE THAN ONE FILE IS CHECKED IN BLOCK 1. Except for Revolutionary War service, these are two different files and must be searched separately.

☐ REQUIRED MINIMUM IDENTIFICATION OF VETERAN WAS NOT PROVIDED. Please complete blocks 2 (give full name), 3, 4, and 5 and resubmit your order.

☐ MORE THAN ONE VETERAN'S NAME appears in Block 2.

☐ THE FILES YOU REQUESTED ABOVE ARE NOT IN THE CUSTODY OF THE NATIONAL ARCHIVES. There are no bounty land warrant applications for service after 1855. We do not have pensions based on Confederate service. Please see the reverse of the instruction sheet for this form or the attached leaflets or information sheets.

Sample of NATF Form 85 for copies of Federal (Union) Pensions. *Courtesy of the National Archives and Records Administration.*

National Archives Reproduction Schedules

G183851 NATIONAL ARCHIVES ORDER FOR COPIES OF MILITARY SERVICE RECORDS
(See Instructions page before completing this form)

If we locate the record you request below, we will copy it for you. The cost for these copies is $17.
Indicate your preferred method of payment at the bottom of this page. There is no charge for an unsuccessful search.

SECTION A. REQUIRED MINIMUM IDENTIFICATION OF VETERAN - MUST BE COMPLETED OR YOUR ORDER CANNOT BE SERVICED

1. VETERAN (Give last, first, and middle names)

◆ *Please note: ARMY SERVICE ONLY. See reverse of instructions page for information about Navy and Marine Corps service.*

2. STATE FROM WHICH HE SERVED

3. WAR IN WHICH, OR DATES BETWEEN WHICH, HE SERVED

4. IF SERVICE WAS CIVIL WAR,
☐ UNION   ☐ CONFEDERATE

PLEASE PROVIDE THE FOLLOWING ADDITIONAL INFORMATION, IF KNOWN

5. UNIT IN WHICH HE SERVED (Name of regiment or number, company, etc., name of ship)

6. IF SERVICE WAS ARMY, ARM IN WHICH HE SERVED
☐ INFANTRY   ☐ CAVALRY   ☐ ARTILLERY   If other, specify:

7. Rank
☐ OFFICER   ☐ ENLISTED

8. KIND OF SERVICE
☐ VOLUNTEER   ☐ REGULARS

9. DATE OF BIRTH

10. PLACE OF BIRTH (City, County, State, etc.)

11. DATE OF DEATH

12. PLACE OF DEATH (City, County, State, etc.)

SECTION B. THIS SPACE IS FOR OUR REPLY TO YOU. PLEASE GO TO SECTION C.

We were unable to search for the file you requested above. No payment is required. Your request is returned because:

☐ REQUIRED MINIMUM IDENTIFICATION OF VETERAN WAS NOT PROVIDED. Please complete blocks 1 (give full name), 2, 3, and 4 and resubmit your order.

☐ See attached forms, leaflets, or information sheets.

Sample of NATF Form 86 for copies of military service records (Union or Confederate). *Courtesy of the National Archives and Records Administration.*

Fair Oaks, Va. Lt. James B. Washington, a Confederate prisoner, with Capt. George A. Custer of the 5th Cavalry, U.S.A. *James F. Gibson, 1862 May 31. Library of Congress, Prints & Photographs Division (LC-B8171-0428)*

7

Officers of the Union and the Confederacy

Union Officers

Heitman, Francis B. *Historical Register and Dictionary of the United States Army 1789-1903.*, 2 volumes. Washington, DC: US Government Printing Office, 1903.

Hewett, Janet B., editor. *The Roster of Union Soldiers.* 33 Volumes. Wilmington, NC: Broadfoot Publishing Co., 1998.

Warner, Ezra J. *Generals in Blue: Lives of the Union Commanders*. Baton Rouge, LA: Louisiana University Press, 1977.

Confederate Officers

Carroll, John M. *List of Field Officers, Regiments & Battalions of the Confederate States Army* 1861-1865. Mattituck, New York: J.M. Carroll & Company, 1983.

Locating Union and Confederate Records

Watts, John. N.Y. Surg 3 art 6 July 1812; resd 15 Apr 1813.

Watts, Joshua Howe. Ind. N Mex. Addl paymr vols 30 June 1862; bvt lt col vols 13 Mar 1865 for fai and mer ser; hon must out 1 June 1869.

Watts, Richard. Va. Va. Ens 35 inf 5 Apr 1814; 3 lt 25 June 1814; hon dischd 15 June 1815.

Watts, Richard K. Md. 2 lt 36 inf 30 Apr 1813; 1 lt 1 May 1814; r paymr Nov 1814 to June 1815; hon dischd 15 June 1815.

Watts, Robert. N Y. Capt 41 inf 31 July 1813; resd — Sept 1813.

Watts, William M. Pa. Pa. 2 lt 3 cav 19 Feb 1862; 1 lt 11 Mar 1863; resd 27 July 1863; pvt I 7 Pa cav 27 Feb 1864. 1 lt adjt 15 May 1865; hon must out 23 Aug 1865.

was "Resolved unanimously, That the thanks of congs be presented to brig gen Wayne for his brave prudent and soldierly con in the spirited and well-conducted attack on Stony Point; that a gold medal emblematical of this action be struck and presented to brig gen Wayne;" bvt maj gen 30 Sept 1783; served to close of war; maj gen and commander U S A 5 Mar 1792; died 15 Dec 1796.

Wayne, Henry Constantine. Ga. Ga. Cadet M A 1 July 1834 (14); 2 lt 4 art 1 July 1838; tr to 1 art 12 July 1838; 1 lt 16 May 1842 to 22 Feb 1851; capt a q m 11 May 1846; bvt maj 20 Aug 1847 for gal and mer con in the battles of Contreras and Churubusco Mex; resd 31 Dec 1860; (brig gen C S A war 1861 to 1865; died 16 Mar 1883.)

Wayne, Richard. Ga. Ga. Asst surg 13 July 1832: resd 31 Jan 1834.

Heitman, Francis B. *Historical Register and Dictionary of the United States Army 1789-1903.*, 2 Volumes. Washington, D.C.: U.S. Government Printing Office, 1903

Waymack, John VA 15th Cav. Co.K	Wayne, H.C. LA 17th Inf. Co.B
Waymack, M. AR 13th Mil. Co.A	Wayne, Henry VA 19th Cav. Co.A
Waymack, Micajah AR 18th Inf. Co.H Cpl.	Wayne, Henry A. GA 38th Inf. Co.B
Waymack, Shadrach W. VA 15th Inf. Co.G Sgt.	Wayne, Henry C. Gen. & Staff Maj.Gen.
Waymack, William AR 18th Inf. Co.H	Wayne, J. NC 44th Inf. Co.F
Wayman, Belfield C. VA 7th Inf. Co.K 1st Sgt.	Wayne, J.A. KY 3rd Mtd.Inf. Co.A
Wayman, Edward VA Cav. Mosby's Regt. (Part.Rangers) Co.C	Wayne, J.A. 3rd Conf.Inf. Co.D Sgt.
	Wayne, Jack AL 16th Inf. Co.A
Wayman, F. Luther MO Arty. Jos. Bledsoe's Co. Sgt.	Wayne, J.A.J. GA 8th Inf. (St.Guards) Co.F 1st Lt.
Wayman, James W. VA 4th Cav. Co.D	Wayne, James VA 55th Inf. Co.G
Wayman, John NC McMillan's Co.	Wayne, J.B. GA Cherokee Legion (St.Guards) Co.A
Wayman, John J. VA 4th Cav. Co.D	

Hewett, Janet B., editor. *The Roster of Confederate Soldiers 1861-1865, 16 Volumes.* Wilmington, N.C.: Broadfoot Publishing Co., 1996.

Henry Constantine Wayne was born in Savannah, Georgia, on September 18, 1815. He received his early education in the schools of Northampton and Cambridge, Massachusetts. In 1834 he was appointed to West Point and was graduated in 1838 as a 2nd lieutenant in the 4th Artillery. He transferred to the quartermaster's department in 1846 with rank of staff captain; he was Georgia, he was appointed adjutant and inspector general of the state by Governor Joseph E. Brown. On December 16, 1861 Wayne was commissioned a brigadier general in the Provisional Army of the Confederate States. However, four days after being ordered to Joseph E. Johnston at Manassas Junction (January 7, 1862), he resigned his Confederate commission. He then served until the end of the

Warner, Ezra J. *Generals in Gray: Lives of the Confederate Commanders. New Orleans, LA: Louisiana University Press.*

Carroll, John M. *List of Staff Officers of the Confederate States Army* 1861-1865. Mattituck, New York: J.M. Carroll & Company, 1983.

Hewett, Janet B., editor. *The Roster of Confederate Soldiers 1861-1865*, 16 Volumes. Wilmington, N.C.: Broadfoot Publishing Co., 1996.

Krick, Robert K. *Lee's Colonels*. 4th edition. Dayton, Ohio: The Press of Morningside Bookshop, 1992.

Warner, Ezra J. *Generals in Gray: Lives of the Confederate Commanders*. Baton Rouge, LA: Louisiana University Press, 1981.

Wright, Marcus J. *General Officers of the Confederate Army*. Mattituck, NY: J.M. Carrol & Company, Mattituck & Bryan, 1983.

Union and Confederate Navy Officers

Donnelly, Ralph W. *Biographical Sketches of the Commissioned Officers of the Confederate States Marine Corps*. Washington, NC: Ralph W. Donnelly, 1983.

Callahan, Edward W., ed. *List of Officers of the Navy of the United States and of the Marine Corps, from 1775 to 1900*. New York: L.R. Hamersly & Co., 1901.

Official Records of the Union and Confederate Navies in the War of the Rebellion: General Index. Washington, D.C.: Navy Department, 1927. (Consists in part of a personal name index to 30 volumes of transcripts of official records.)

Office of Naval Records and Library. *Register of the Confederate States Navy, 1861-1865*. Washington, D.C.: Navy Department, 1931. (Identifies Confederate naval officers alphabetically by surname.)

Office of Naval Records and Library United States Navy Department. *Register of Officers of the Confederate States Navy, 1861-1865.* Mattituck, NY: J.M Carroll & Company, Bryan & Mattituck, 1983.

Powell, William H. editor. *Officers of the Army and Navy (Regular) Who Served in the Civil War.* Philadelphia, PA: L.R. Hamersly & Co., 1892.

Powell, William H. editor. *Officers of the Army and Navy (Volunteer) Who Served in the Civil War.* Philadelphia, PA: L.R. Hamersly & Co., 1893.

Unidentified Union volunteer with shouldered rifle and bayonet in photographer's studio. *Library of Congress, Prints & Photographs Division (LC-B8172-1174)*

8

Compiled Records Showing Service of Military Units in Volunteer Union Organizations

Record of Events—Union

Beginning in 1890, the War Department compiled histories of the *volunteer* military organizations that served during the Civil War. The compiled records for each organization are in jackets or envelopes bearing the title "Record of Events" which help the researcher learn additional information about the soldier's war activities. The records are compiled from information on the original muster rolls and returns, and the quantity of information varies on each unit. The records rarely name individual soldiers, but the records are descriptions of the activities and movements of the company. The abstracts relate to the stations, movements, or activities of each unit or part of it. Frequently there is information about the unit's organization or composition, strength and losses, and disbanding. The "Record of Events" can be used in conjunction with the soldier's CMSR and pension file to determine what the soldier's unit was doing during his participation. For an example of a Compiled Record of Organizations, see the example in Chapter 9.

Compiled Records Showing Service of Military Units in Volunteer Union Organizations (M594) 225 rolls

RECORD OF EVENTS—UNION (M594)*

STATE	NATIONAL ARCHIVES ROLLS (M 594)	FHLMICROFILM #
Alabama	1	1488453
Arizona	1	1488453
Arkansas	1	1488453
California	2-3	1488454 - 1488455
Colorado	4	1488456
Connecticut	5-8	1488457 - 1488460
Dakota Territory	9	1488461
Delaware	9	1488461
Washington D.C.	10	1488462
Florida	10	1488462
Georgia	10	1488462
Illinois	11-33	1488463 - 1488485
Indiana	34-49	1488486 - 1488501
Iowa	50-57	1488502 - 1488509
Kansas	58-59	1488510 - 1488518
Kentucky	60-66	1488518
Louisiana	67	1488519
Maine	68-71	1488520 - 1488523
Massachusetts	75-82	1488527 - 1488534
Michigan	83-89	1488535 - 1488541
Minnesota	90-91	1488542 - 1488543
Mississippi	91	1488543
Missouri	92-100	1488544 - 1488553
Nevada	101	1488553
Nebraska	101	1488553
New Hampshire	101-103	1488553 - 1488555
New Jersey	104-107	1488556 - 1588559
New Mexico	107	1488559
New York	108-139	1488560 - 1488591

North Carolina	139	1488591
Ohio	140-163	1488592 - 1488615
Oregon	163	1488615
Pennsylvania	164-185	1488616 - 1488637
Rhode Island	186-187	1488638 - 1488639
Tennessee	188-190	1488640 - 1488642
Texas	190	1488642
Vermont	191-193	1488643 - 1488645
Virginia	193	1488645
Washington Terr.	193	1488645
West Virginia	194-196	1488646 - 1488648
Wisconsin	197-203	1488649 - 1488655
US Colored Troops	204-217	1488672 - 1488669
US Volunteers	218-219	1488670 - 1488671
US Veteran Corps	219-225	1488672 - 1488677
Other US Organizations	225	1488677

*To order HeritageQuest films in Series M594 see chapter 22.

Book

Hewett, Janet B., editor. *The Supplement to the Army Official Records, 100 volumes.* Wilmington, NC: Broadfoot Publishing Co., 2000. This series contains the *Compiled Records Showing Service of Military Units in Volunteer Union Organizations* which are organized by State and then by Unit and will be available in libraries and archives.

Portrait of an unidentified soldier who appears to be a Confederate.
Library of Congress, Prints & Photographs Division (LC-B8184-10692).
From Mr. G.K. Holmes, Cornwall Bridge, Conn.

9

Compiled Records Showing Service of Military Units in Confederate Organizations

Record of Events—Confederate

In 1903, the War Department compiled abstract histories of the movements and activities of the Confederate Military Units. Original muster rolls and returns were the principal sources of information. Rosters, payrolls, hospital registers, casualty lists, Union prison registers and rolls, parole rolls, and inspection reports were also abstracted. Because many of the Confederate Army records were lost or destroyed by the end of the war, the histories of most of the units are incomplete. The quantity of information varies on each unit. The records rarely name individual soldiers, but are descriptions of the activities and movements of the company. The abstracts relate to the stations, movements, or activities of each unit or part of it. Frequently there is information about the unit's organization or composition, strength and losses, and disbanding. The "Record of Events" can be used in conjunction with the soldier's CMSR and pension file to determine what the soldier's unit was doing during his participation. National Archives M861, 74 rolls *Confederate Marines and Navy are not included.*

RECORD OF EVENTS—CONFEDERATE (M861)*

STATE	NATIONAL ARCHIVES ROLLS (M861)	FHL MICROFILM #
Alabama	rolls 1-5	1380856 - 1380860
Arizona	roll 5	1380860
Arkansas	rolls 6-9	1380861 - 1380864
Florida	rolls 10-11	1380865 - 1380866
Georgia	rolls 12-19	1380867 - 1380874
Kentucky	rolls 20-21	1380875 - 1380876
Louisiana	rolls 22-26	1380877 - 1380881
Maryland	roll 26	1380881
Mississippi	rolls 27-33	1380882 -1380889
Missouri	rolls 34-36	1380889 - 1380891
North Carolina	rolls 37-42	1380892 - 1380897
South Carolina	rolls 43-48	1380898 - 1380903
Tennessee	rolls 49-55	1380904 - 1380910
Texas	rolls 56-61	1380911 - 1380916
Virginia	rolls 62-72	1380917 - 1380927
Organized Directly by the Confederate Government	rolls 73-74	1380928 - 1380929

*To order HeritageQuest films in Series M861 see chapter 22.

Book

Hewett, Janet B., editor. *The Supplement to the Army Official Records, 100 volumes.* Wilmington, NC: Broadfoot Publishing Co., 2000.

This series contains the *Compiled Records Showing Service of Military Units in Confederate Organizations* which are organized by State and then by Unit and will be available in libraries and archives.

Compiled Records Showing Service of Confederate Organizations

Field & Staff, 13 Reg't *Iowa Inf.*

Field and Staff Muster Roll

for *July & Aug.* 1864

shows station,

Near Jonesboro Ga.

RECORD OF EVENTS.

June 30th to July 2nd front Kenesaw Mt. July 3. 4. 5: + 6" engag-
ing the enemy on Nickojack-
Creek: 10" occupy their works
the Chattahoochee river, July 16.
to 19 moved through Marietta,
Roswell and Decatur to Atlanta and
Augusta R.R. July 20: 21: + 22"
and engagement with the enemy-
very loss. July 28" reinforced 15th
A.C. engaged with the enemy. July 29th
Aug. 26: skirmishing and Picketing
in front of Atlanta Sep. 1 skirmishing
with the enemy south of Atlanta over
Flint River. Aug. 2nd moved to Love-
July & returned to East Point Ga.
Total loss in Battles in July.
Aug. 309. Com. officers and
listed men.

French.

(Confederate.)

Field & Staff, 1 Reg't *Ky Inf*

Field and Staff Muster Roll

of the organization named above,

for *Nov & Dec* , 1861,

shows station of Field and Staff,

Camp Near Centerville Va

RECORD OF EVENTS.

Friday Nov 8 marched as
an advance guard to outpost
No 7 distant about 2 miles
from Centerville & returned
Nov 11 November 23 went
to outpost No 8 on picket
duty 2½ miles North east
of Centerville. returned Nov
26. Dec 8 went to outpost
No 8 again & returned 11th
Friday Morning Dec 20 the
Regiment left Camp at an
early hour and after a
rapid march of about 18
miles engaged the enemy
near Drainsville in a dense
pine thicket - the fight lasted
for more than one hour
when under orders the Reg't
fell back to Herndon Station
on the London and Hampshire R R
and from thence returning to Camp.

A. W. Crosby.

(0186)

Compiled records showing Service of Military Units in Volunteer Organizations
and Compiled Records Showing Service of Military Units in Confederate
Organizations. *Washington, D.C.: National Archives.*

2d Rhode Island Infantry. *Library of Congress, Prints & Photographs Division (LC-USZ62-99873)*

10

Regimental Histories

Union

Dornbusch, Charles E., Compiler. *Military Bibliography of the Civil War.* 3 volumes, 1961-72. Dayton, Ohio: The Press of Morningside Bookshop, 1987. (Union and Confederate)

Dyer, Frederick H. *Compendium of the Rebellion.* 2 volumes 1908. Reprint. Dayton, Ohio: The Press of Morningside Bookshop, 1978. (Union)

Confederate

Compiled Records Showing Service of Military Units in Confederate Organization. National Archives Microfilm Publication M861. Family History Library microfilm numbers 1380856-1380929.

Crute, Joseph H., Jr. *Units of the Confederate States Army.* Midlothian, Virginia: Derwent Books, 1987.

Dornbusch, Charles E., Compiler. *Military Bibliography of the Civil War.* 3 volumes, 1961-72. Dayton, Ohio: The Press of Morningside Bookshop, 1987. (Union and Confederate)

Locating Union and Confederate Records

rdon's Mills September 11-13. Battle of Chick-
September 19-20. Siege of Chattanooga, Tenn.,
ber 24-October 26. Moved to Bridgeport, Ala.,
26, and duty there till January 24, 1864. At
ih, Tenn., till May. Atlanta (Ga.) Campaign May
mber 8. Tunnel Hill May 6-7. Demonstrations
ky Faced Ridge and Dalton May 8-13. Buzzard's
3ap May 8-9. Battle of Resaca May 14-15. Near
>n May 18-19. Near Cassville May 19. Advance
las May 22-25. Operations on line of Pumpkin
·eek and battles about Dallas, New Hope Church
latoona Hills May 25-June 5. Operations about
a and against Kenesaw Mountain June 10-July 2.
ill June 11-14. Lost Mountain June 15-17. As-
ı Kenesaw June 27. Ruff's Station, Smyrna Camp
, July 4. Chattahoochie River July 5-17. Peach
·eek July 19-20. Siege of Atlanta July 22-August
ink movement on Jonesboro August 25-30. Bat-
onesboro August 31-September 1. Lovejoy Sta-
·ptember 2-6. Duty at Atlanta till October 3.
ɔns against Hood in North Georgia and North
a October 3-November 3. Moved to Pulaski,
Nashville Campaign November-December. Co-
Duck River, November 24-27. Battle of Frank-
ember 30. Battle of Nashville December 15-16.
of Hood to the Tennessee River December 17-
>ved to Huntsville, Ala., and duty there till
1865. Operations in East Tennessee March 15-
:. Moved to Nashville, Tenn., and duty there till
Mustered out June 13, and discharged at Camp

Guarding Railroad Bridge at Opequan till December 20.
Ordered to Martinsburg December 30, and duty there
till March 17, 1865. Moved to Cumberland, Md., March
17, thence to Winchester April 5, and duty there till
June 2. At Cumberland, Md., till June 24. Mustered
out June 24, 1865.

Regiment lost during service 3 Officers and 60 Enlisted men killed and mortally wounded and 3 Officers
and 87 Enlisted men by disease. Total 153.

92nd REGIMENT INFANTRY.

Organized at Camp Marietta and at Gallipolis, Ohio,
August-September, 1862. (Cos. "A," "B" and "C" gar-
rison duty at Gallipolis, Ohio, September.) Ordered to
Point Pleasant, Va., October 7, 1862. Attached to Dis-
trict of the Kanawha, W. Va., Dept. of the Ohio, to De-
cember, 1862. 2nd Brigade, Kanawha Division, W. Va.,
Dept. Ohio, to February, 1863. Crook's Brigade, Baird's
Division, Army of Kentucky, Dept. of the Cumberland,
to June, 1863. 3rd Brigade, 4th Division, 14th Army
Corps, Army of the Cumberland, to October, 1863. 1st
Brigade, 3rd Division, 14th Army Corps, to June, 1865.

SERVICE.—March to Charleston, W. Va., October 14-
November 16, 1862. Duty at Camp Vinton till January
1, 1863. Moved to Tompkin's Farm and Colesworth
January 1-3. Moved to Nashville, Tenn., January 7-22,
and duty there till February 17. Moved to Carthage,
Tenn., February 17, and duty there till June 5. Moved
to Murfreesboro, Tenn., June 5. Middle Tennessee or
Tullahoma Campaign June 23-July 7. Hoover's Gap

Frederick, H. Dyer. Compendium of the Rebellion. *2 Volumes, 1908. Reprint.*
(Dayton, Ohio: The Press of Morningside Bookshop, 1978) 1537.

---

22. VIRGINIA 20TH HEAVY ARTILLERY BATTALION

Organization: Organized with four companies on June 21, 1862, per S.O.
#143, Adjutant and Inspector General's Office. Surrendered at Appomattox
Court House, Virginia, on April 9, 1865.

First Commander: Arthur S. Cunningham (Lieutenant Colonel) (tempo-
rary)

Field Officers: Johnston DeLagnel (Major)
James E. Robertson (Major)

Assignments: 2nd Division, Inner Line, Richmond Defenses, Department of
  Richmond (May 1863-December 1864)
Artillery Defenses, Department of Richmond (December 1864-April 1865)
Crutchfield's Brigade, G. W. C. Lee's Division, Army of Northern Virginia
  (April 1865)

Battles: Petersburg Siege (June 1864-April 1865)
Sayler's Creek (April 6, 1865)
Appomattox Court House (April 9, 1865)

23. VIRGINIA 28TH HEAVY ARTILLERY BATTALION
See: VIRGINIA 28TH INFANTRY BATTALION

Stewart Sifakis. Compendium of the Confederate Armies.
5 Volumes. (New York: Facts on File, 1992) 9.

Hydrick, Blair D., Compiler. *Civil War Unit Histories. Regimental Histories and Personal Narratives: Part 1: The Confederate States of America and Border States.* Edited by Robert E. Lester. Bethesda, MD: University Publications of America, 1992.

Sifakis, Stewart. *Compendium of the Confederate Armies.* 5 Volumes. New York: Facts on File, 1992.

FHL Catalog

More is available through the FHL Locality Catalog:

UNITED STATES - MILITARY RECORDS - CIVIL WAR, 1861-1865 - REGIMENTAL HISTORIES

[STATE] - MILITARY RECORDS - CIVIL WAR, 1861-1865 - REGIMENTAL HISTORIES.

Periodical Source Index—PERSI

The CD-ROM Periodical Source Index based upon the Allen County Public Libraries' Periodical collection, contains articles on many regimental histories and should not be overlooked. It is easy to use. The material can be looked up by location, record type (Military) then Regimental History for keyword.

Civil War Unit Histories:
Regimental Histories and Personal Narratives

Available through the Family History Library as well as many other major research facilities is the collection of the microfiche edition of *Civil War Unit Histories: Regimental Histories and Personal Narratives.* The microfiche collection is produced by University Publications of America, Bethesda, MD, and is a collection divided into five units by states. The Family History Library has "A Guide to the Microfiche Edition of Civil War

Unit Histories: Regimental Histories and Personal Narrative: Parts 1 to 4, Edited by Robert E. Lester Call number is 973, M2cwu. The Units Histories and narratives are divided into the following States in the Family History Library's collection of 6,347 microfiche.

PART	REGION	STATES INCLUDED
1	Confederate States	AL, AR, FL, GA, KY, LA, MD, MS, MO, NC, SC, TN, TX, VA and higher and independent Commands of the Confederate Navy
2	New England States	CT, ME, MA, NH, RI, VT
3	Mid Atlantic States	NY, PA, NJ, DE, D.C., WV
4	Midwest and West	IL, IN, IA, KS, MI, MN, OH, WI, CA, CO, Dakota Terr, NE, NV, NM, OR, WA
5	Union	Higher and Independent Commands and Naval Forces of the Union

Regimental Histories of the American Civil War

HeritageQuest films are available for this series of 1,084 monographic titles in microfiche format, titled *Regimental Histories of the American Civil War*. The compilation and filming of this series was based upon C. E. Dornbusch's *Military Bibliography of the Civil War, Volumes I and II: Regimental and Personal Narratives of the Civil War.* This series may be found in many libraries including Sutro in California. The histories, monographs and personal narratives were all published up to about 1916. Following is a brief guide to the series for 7,255 microfiche.

UNIT 1 - NEW ENGLAND STATES (220 TITLES / 1,139 FICHE)

Connecticut	32 titles/124 fiche
Maine	30 titles/202 fiche
Massachusetts	101 titles/487 fiche
New Hampshire	23 titles/149 fiche
Rhode Island	22 titles/111 fiche

Vermont   12 titles/66 fiche

UNIT 2 - MID-ATLANTIC STATES (225 TITLES / 1,567 FICHE)

Delaware   3 titles/ 7 fiche
New Jersey   16 titles/85 fiche
New York   119 titles/1,042 fiche
Pennsylvania   87 titles/422 fiche

UNIT 3 - MID-WEST STATES (330 TITLES / 1,590 FICHE)

Illinois	74 titles/335 fiche	Michigan	25 titles/175 fiche
Indiana	50 titles/335 fiche	Minnesota	8 titles/40 fiche
Iowa	37 titles/231 fiche	Ohio	101 titles/437 fiche
Kansas	3 titles/12 fiche	Wisconsin	32 titles/125 fiche

UNIT 4 - BORDER AND WESTERN STATES (88 TITLES / 339 FICHE)

Arkansas	4 titles/8 fiche	Missouri	14 titles/46 fiche
California	8 titles/22 fiche	Nebraska	1 title/3 fiche
Colorado	2 titles/4 fiche	Nevada	1 title/1 fiche
District of Columbia	2 titles/6 fiche	Tennessee	18 titles/72 fiche
Kentucky	19 titles/102 fiche	West Virginia	8 titles/35 fiche
Maryland	11 titles/40 fiche		

UNIT 5 - CONFEDERATE STATES (217 TITLES / 712 FICHE)

Alabama	18 titles/61 fiche	North Carolina	29 titles/128 fiche
Florida	3 titles/9 fiche	South Carolina	28 titles/91 fiche
Georgia	18 titles/50 fiche	Texas	17 titles/49 fiche
Louisiana	12 titles/82 fiche	Virginia	82 titles/224 fiche
Mississippi	10 titles/18 fiche		

UNIT 6 - REFERENCE WORKS (4 TITLES / 1,909 FICHE)

The Official Records of the Union and Confederate Armies in the War of the Rebellion (1,482 fiche)

Personal narratives of events in the War of the Rebellion, being papers read, before the Rhode Island Soldiers' and Sailors' Historical Society (65 fiche)

Official records of the Union and Confederate Navies in the War of the Rebellion (316 fiche)

Official Army register of the volunteer force of the United States Army for The years 1861, '62, '63, '64, '65 (44 fiche)

Andersonville Prison, Ga. Issuing rations. *1864 August 17.*
National Archives and Records Administration

11

Union
Prisoners of War

National Archives RG 249—Commissary General of Prisoners, 17 June 1862-19 August 1867.

The records were transferred to the Office of the Adjutant General and the records include:

Register of Troops Captured by the Enemy

Register of Federal Prisoners of War Confined in Confederate Prisons 1861-1864

Register of Federal Prisoners of War From Confederate Authorities.

Register of Settled Claims for Money Taken from Federal Prisoners in Confederate Prisons, 1866-67

Name Index to Records of Paroles, Exchanges, and Deaths of Federal Prisoners of War

Confederate Prisons
where Union Soldiers were incarcerated

Belle Island–Richmond, Virginia

Cahaba Prison (Castle Morgan)–Cahaba, Alabama

Camp Florence–Florence, South Carolina

Camp Ford—Tyler, Texas

Camp Groce–Hempstead, Texas

Camp Lawton–Millen, Georgia

Libby Prison–Richmond, Virginia

Camp Oglethorpe–Macon, Georgia

Camp Sumter–Andersonville, Georgia

Castle Pickney–Charleston, South Carolina

Castle Thunder–Petersburg, Virginia

Crews Prision–Petersburg, Virginia

Danville's Prisons–Danville, Virginia

Fort Norfolk–Norfolk, Virginia

Liggons Prison–Richmond, Virginia

Salisbury Prison–Salisbury, North Carolina

FHL Catalog

More is available through the Family History Library Locality Catalog:

UNITED STATES - MILITARY RECORDS - CIVIL WAR, 1861-1865 - PRISONERS AND PRISONS.

[STATE] - MILITARY RECORDS - CIVIL WAR, 1861-1865 - PRISONERS AND PRISONS.

Compiled Military Service Records

Another possible source for prison records is his Compiled Military Service Record. The Compiled Military Service Record states where and when he was held as prisoner—see chapter 4.

Samuel Harrop, compiled military service record
(Corporal, 91st Ohio Infantry, Co. B) *Washington D.C.: National Archives.*

Gettysburg, Pa. Three Confederate prisoners. *1863 July. Library of Congress, Prints & Photographs Division (LC-B8171-2288)*

12

Confederate Prisoners of War

Selected Records of the War Department Relating to Confederate Prisoners of War (M598)

CONTENTS	NATIONAL ARCHIVES ROLL (M598)*	FHL MICROFILM #
Registers of prisoners submitted by the commissary general of prisoners (roll 4 lists deaths)	1-6	1303301 - 1303306
Registers of prisoners submitted by the commissary general of prisoners (roll 8 lists applications and approvals for release)	7-8	1303307 - 1303308
Registers of unclaimed money, effect of deceased soldiers, permits for furnishing of clothing to prisoners, deaths.	9	1303309
Registers of deaths compiled by the surgeon general; arranged by state	10-12	1303310 - 1303312
Registers of prisons (See roll 1 for a listing of the prisons that submitted volumes of records and numbers of the rolls on which they are found.)	13-139	1303313 - 1303439
Division of West Mississippi	140-142	1303440
District of West Tennessee-provost marshal	143	1303443
Records relating to various prisons	144-145	1303444 - 1303445

*To order HeritageQuest films in Series M598 see chapter 22.

Locating Union and Confederate Records

Name	Rank. Co.	Regiment.	Date of Death.	Locality of Grave.
		POINT LOOKOUT, MD.		
Hunter, John,	Pvt. H	36 Va.	Feb. 21, 1865.	Confederate Cemetery.
Huree, William,	H	10 Ga. Inf.	Nov. 19, 1863.	"
Hursey, G. A.,	Corp. H	8 Ala. Inf.	Nov. 19,	"
Hutchinson, J. J.,	Pvt. A	22 Va.	April 20, 1865.	"
Hutchinson, J. L.,	" G	3 Va.	March 31,	"
Hutchinson, Thos.,	" I	24 Va.	May 31,	"
Hutchison, M.,	" O	6 S. C. Cav.	Jan. 9,	"
Hyatt, R. A. L.,	" E	Thomas' N. C. Legion.	Jan. 13,	"
Hyde, Samuel L.,	" D	20 Miss. Inf.	Sept. 2, 1864.	"
Hylton, Jeremiah,	" B	42 Va. Inf.	Jan. 6,	"
Ingles, Geo. A.,	Pvt. F	22 Va.	Dec. 31, 1864.	Confederate Cemetery.
Ingold, J. A.,	" A	53 N. C. Inf.	Dec. 10, 1863.	"
Ingram, J.,	" C	16 Ga.	Sept. 27, 1864.	"
Ingram, Wm.,	" K	18 N. C. Inf.	Nov. 9, 1863.	"
Inman, Alexander,	" E	3 (40) N. C. Art.	March 9, 1865.	"
Inman, J. A.,	" G	5 Va. Cav.	Sept. 13, 1864.	"
Insce, D. B.,	" K	12 N. C. Inf.	Nov. 30,	"
Insce, Henry,	" K	12 N. C. Inf.	Nov. 7,	"
Ipock, Albert,	Sgt. O	3 (40) N. C. Art.	Feb. 18, 1865.	"
Irick, W. M.,	Pvt. K	5 S. C. Cav.	Jan. 29,	"
Irwin, G. H.,	" E	3 Ala. Cav.	Nov. 1, 1863.	"
Isbell, Robt. G.,	" B	15 Ga. Inf.	Dec. 10, 1864.	"
Isdel, J. T.,	" C	59 Ga. Inf.	Oct. - 1863.	"
Isham, Nathan,	" A	Winis N. C. Battn.	Jan. 7, 1865.	"
Isley, John,	" E	1 N. C.	Aug. 8, 1864.	"
Ivey, W. L.,	" A	30 N. C. Inf.	Jan. 26, 1865.	"
Jack, John H.,	Pvt. K	52 Va. Inf.	March 27, 1864.	Confederate Cemetery.
Jackson, David,	" K	60 Tenn.	Oct. - 1863.	"
Jackson, Henry,	" B	16 Va. Cav.	Jan. 24, 1865.	"
Jackson, J. A.,	" B	7 S. C. Cav.	April 24, 1864.	"
Jackson, John M.,	" G	22 N. C. Inf.	June 27,	"
Jackson, Leadbarte,	" E	3 Va. Cav.	June 24, 1865.	"
Jackson, Peter,		Batty. B, Stiles' Ga. Art.	May 29,	"
Jackson, Thomas P.,	" K	1 Ky. Cav.	Sept. 18, 1864.	"
Jackson, Wm.,	" A	14 Va. Inf.	Nov. 10, 1863.	"
Jackson, Wm. O.,	" F	14 Va.	Jan. 27, 1865.	"
James, A. F.,	Corp. B	13 S. C.	Oct. 22, 1864.	"
James, Geo. T.,	Pvt. H	36 Va.	June 2, 1865.	"

Registers of Confederate Soldiers, Sailors, and Citizens Who Died in Federal Prisons and Military Hospitals in the North, 1861-1865. *National Archives Microfilm Publication M918.*

Registers of Confederate Soldiers, Sailors, and Citizens Who Died in Federal Prisons and Military Hospitals in the North, National Archives M918 — one roll of microfilm, Family History Library Microfilm 1024456, lists arranged alphabetically by location of the death, then by the name of the soldier. *Family Tree Maker's Family Archive #119: Military Records: Confederate Soldiers 1861-1865.* This CD contains the complete contents of National Archive microfilm roll number M918 indexing the names of approximately 25,000 individuals and is indexed by name. The data includes: name, rank, company, regiment, death date, location of death or burial, number and locality of grave. Both of these items are available from the HeritageQuest store. See chapter 22 for ordering information.

Confederate Naval and Marine Personnel Records (National Archives M260)

Hospital and Prison records, Navy and Marines, Family History Library microfilm numbers 191662-191668. See chapter 22 to order this item from the HeritageQuest store.

Civil War Union Prisons where Confederates were Imprisoned

Alton Prison—Alton, Illinois

Camp Bulter—Springfield, Illinois

Camp Chase—Columbus, Ohio

Camp Douglas—Chicago, Illinois

Camp Morton—Indianapolis, Indiana

Camp Parole—Annapolis, Maryland

Camp Randall—Madison, Wisconsin

Carroll Prison—Point Lookout, Maryland

David's Island—New York, New York

Locating Union and Confederate Records

Surname	Christian Name	Rank	Co.	Regiment	Disease or Wound	Date of Death	Place of Death
						1863	
Chrisler	Edward	Pvt	16		Illness Selep	Feby 6	Murfreesboro
Bray	John			Inf'try		"	Nashville Tenn
Bryant	Robert			Knights Batt'y	Febris Typhoidus	"	"
Bibby	Charles			Cav. 11	Variola	" 11	Alton Ill
Bullard	James			McLd	"	6	
Bear	William H			Portess	"	" 14	
Brown	John			Battalion	"	" 16	
Brown	Israel			Jenkins	"	" 18	
Bloom or	Stephen					" 10	St Louis Mo
Duncan	Henry					" 12	
Butler Batt	J. C.					" 27	Burnett Kent
Black	J. C.			Shelton	Bronchitis	" 27	
Bean	M					" 11	St N Charleston
Miller	A. C.	Pvt			Pneumonia	March 9	Cp Douglas Ill
Sergeant	Thomas					" 9	
Burk	J. C.			Crawford	Febris Typhoides	" 18	Cp Douglas Mo
Rowland	James H.					" 28	Springfield
Box	William					" 21	Smallpox
Brown	Thomas				Variola	" 17	St Louis Mo
Byrd	Robert P					" 7	Cap Chase
Buchanan	William				Infl of Lungs	" 20	Memphis Tenn
Brown	Nathan			Brazier	Infl of Lungs	April 25	St Louis Mo
Burke	W. F.	Pvt		Doone	Diarrhea Chr	" 23	"
Baker	David S			Pardubec	" Acuta	" 1	"
Ballard	W. F			Drumington	Febris Typhoides	" 10	Cp Douglas
Braden	J. H				Variola	" 9	St Louis Mo

National Archives M598. Confederate Prisoners of War. Microfilm no. 1303310.
Family History Library, Salt Lake City, Utah.

Elmira Prison—Elmira, New York

Forest Hall Military Prison—Georgetown, DC

Fort Delaware—Delaware

Fort Lafayette—New York, New York

Fort McHenry—Baltimore, Maryland

Fort Warren—Boston, Massachusetts

Gratiot Street Prison—St. Louis, Missouri

Johnson's Island Prison—Sandusky, Ohio

Louisville Prison—Louisville, Kentucky

Mackinac Island—Mackinac Island, Michigan

McClean Barracks—Cincinnati, Ohio

Myrtle Street Prison—St. Louis, Missouri

Old Capitol Prison—Washington, DC

Rock Island Prison—Rock Island, Illinois

Western Penitentiary—Allegheny City, Pennsylvania

Family History Library Catalog

More is available through the Family History Library Locality Catalog:

UNITED STATES - MILITARY RECORDS - CIVIL WAR, 1861-1865 - PRISONERS AND PRISONS.

[STATE] - MILITARY RECORDS - CIVIL WAR, 1861-1865 - PRISONERS AND PRISONS.

Compiled Military Service Records

Another possible source is his Compiled Military Service Record. The Compiled Military Service Record will state where and when he was held as prisoner, see Chapters 4 and 5.

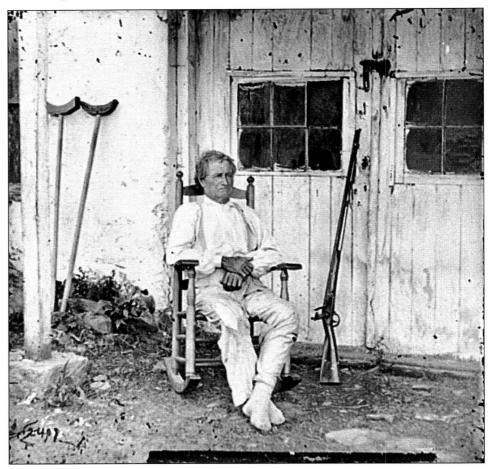

Gettysburg, Pa. John L. Burns, the "old hero of Gettysburg," with gun and crutches. *Timothy H. O'Sullivan, 1863 July. Library of Congress, Prints & Photographs Division (LC-B8171-2402)*

Veteran of Civil War Finally Gets Pension

Pottsville, Pa. — Thomas J. Rose, a Civil war veteran, has finally been given a pension after a clerical error in Washington kept it from him for 50 years. The back pension will amount to several thousands of dollars. Seven congressmen tried to get Rose's record straightened out, but this was not accomplished until the present war led to the discovery of additional records.

"Veteran of Civil War Finally Gets Pension." *Clipping from an unidentified newspaper, ca. 1920. Ohio Historical Society — The African-American Experience in Ohio 1850-1920*

13

Union
Pension Records

General Index to Pension Files, 1861-1934
(National Archives T288)

The federal government issued pensions to soldiers who met certain criteria. Pension files may include information on a soldier's military service, family members, places of residence, and other genealogical information. Most Civil War pensioners were issued to Union Veterans although some Confederate veterans signed a sworn affidavit denouncing their allegiance to the confederacy. After signing the affidavit, they were allowed to apply for pension benefits. Information given in Pension Index: *General Index to Pensions 1861-1934* (National Archives T288) is available through the National Archives and many of it's branch archives. The Pacific-Sierra Regional Office in San Bruno has the series. The Family History Library also has the collection which includes 544 reels of microfilm. The Family History Library microfilm rolls are numbered 540757 through 541300. To order HeritageQuest films in Series T288 see chapter 22.

Other Sources

Veteran's Administration Pension Payment Cards, 1907-1933 (National Archives M850) Family History Library microfilm rolls 1634036-1636574.

Index to Pension Application Files of Remarried Widows Based on Service in Civil War and Later Wars and in the Regular Army after the Civil War.

(3-060 a.)

MILITARY SERVICE.

NAME OF SOLDIER:

Christian O Morbeck

Div.

Ex'r,

No. *122871*   *Oct 15* 189 *2*

SIR:

It is alleged that the above-named man enlisted *22*

Feb, 186 *2*, and served as a

in Co. *F. 15* Reg't *Wis Inf*

also as a _____ in Co. _____ Reg't

_____, and was discharged at _____

on *April* , 18 *65*

No. of prior claim _____

The War Department will please furnish an official statement in this case, showing date of enrollment and date and mode of termination of service.

Very respectfully, *Earl S Lincoln*

THE OFFICER IN CHARGE,
RECORD AND PENSION DIVISION,
WAR DEPARTMENT.

Commissioner.

0—4

War Department,

Record and Pension Division,

OCT 13 1892

Respectfully returned to the

COMMISSIONER OF PENSIONS.

The rolls show that *Christian O. Morbeck*

Co F 15 Mich Inf

mentioned in the preceding indorsement, was enrolled

Feb 2 2 , 186 *2*, and *M O*

a Corp Mar 13 , 186 *5*

as of Co H 15 Wis Inf to which trnsfd

* *See new report*

BY AUTHORITY OF THE SECRETARY OF WAR:

J C Ainsworth
Colonel Major and Surgeon, U. S. Army.
Per *M*.

5269 b—200 m

Christian O. Morbeck. Pension File (Corporal Co. F, 15th Regiment Wisconsin Infantry) *Washington, D.C.: National Archives.*

(National Archives Microcopy M1785). Series M1785 is available from the HeritageQuest store. See chapter 22 for ordering information.

White, Virgil D. *Index to US Military Pension Applications of Remarried Widows for Service Between 1812 and 1911.* Waynesboro, Tennessee: The National Historical Publishing Company, 1999.

Organization Index to Pension Files of Veterans Who Served Between 1861-1900 (National Archives T289)

Family History Library microfilm rolls 1725491-1726255. These are indexed by unit.

Case Files of Disapproved Pension Applications of Widows and Other Dependents of Civil War and Later Navy Veterans (National Archives M1391) Family History Library Fiche Nos. 6333805-6333996.

Book Source

US Pension Bureau. *List of Pensioners on the Roll, Jan 1, 1883.* 5 volumes. Reprint. Baltimore: Genealogical Publishing Company, 1970. Not all veterans were receiving a pension by 1883, some started at later dates.

NATF FORM 85

To receive copies of the actual pension records, request NATF Form 85 by writing to National Archives and Records Administration, General Reference Branch (NNRG), 700 Pennsylvania Ave NW, Washington, D.C. 20408. Forms can be requested via email at *inquire@nara.gov.* Specify "Form 85", the number of forms you need, and send your name and mailing address. When you send for the Pension Record, You may choose between the Full Pension Application File and the Pension Documents Packet. You may want to get the full file as there is often remarkable information included which may not come with the Document only packet. (See the National Archives Reproduction Schedules chapter).

ACT OF JUNE 27, 1890.

APPLICATION FOR INVALID PENSION.

To be executed before a Court of Record or some officer thereof having custody of its seal, or a Notary Public, or a Justice of the Peace, whose official signature shall be verified by his official seal, and in case he has none, his signature and official character shall be certified by a Clerk of the Court of Record, or a City or County Clerk having a seal.

State of _Michigan_, County of _Menominee_, ss.

On this _29th_ day of _May_ A. D. _1902_, personally appeared before me, _Thomas Breen_ a _Justice of the Peace_ within and for the County and State aforesaid, _Christian O. Morbeck_, aged _59_ years, a resident of the _Village_ of _Ingalls_ County of _Menominee_ and State of _Michigan_, who, being duly sworn according to law, declares that he is the identical _Christian O. Morbeck_, who was ENROLLED on the _22d_ day of _February_, 186_2_, in _Co. F. 15th Wis. Inf_ (Here state rank, company and regiment in Military service, or vessel, if in the Navy.) in the service of the United States in the War of the Rebellion, and served at least ninety days, and was HONORABLY DISCHARGED at _Huntsville, Ala_, on the _13th_ day of _March_, 186_5_. That he is _wholly_ (¼, ½, ¾, or totally) unable to earn a support by manual labor by reason of _gunshot wound_ (Here name the disease or injuries from which disabled.) _of left ankle, sciatica, catarrh, bronchitis, disease of eyes, constipation, lumbago, rheumatism and general debility_. That said disabilities are not due to his vicious habits, and are to the best of his knowledge and belief permanent. That he has ____ applied for pension under application No._1123.871_ That he is _not_ a pensioner under Certificate No. ____. (If a pensioner, the Certificate number only need be given.) That he has _not_ been employed in the military or naval service otherwise than as stated above _nor before the 22d day of February 1862_. (Here state what the service was, whether prior or subsequent to that stated above, and the dates at which it began and ended.) That he has not been in the military or naval service of the United States since the _12th_ day of _March_ 186_5_.

That he never in any manner voluntarily engaged in or aided or abetted the late Rebellion against the United States.

That he makes this declaration for the purpose of being placed on the pension roll of the United States, under the provisions of the **Act of June 27, 1890,** _as amended May 9th 1900_

He hereby appoints, with full power of substitution and revocation, _James A. Stephenson_ _Menominee Mich_, his true and lawful attorney to prosecute his claim, the fee to be TEN DOLLARS as prescribed by law. That his POST-OFFICE ADDRESS is _Ingalls_, County of _Menominee_, State of _Michigan_

Christian O. Morbeck
(Claimant's signature.)

Jas. A. Stephenson

Christian O. Morbeck. Pension File (Corporal Co. F, 15th Regiment Wisconsin Infantry) *Washington, D.C.: National Archives.*

Western Div.

3—173.

W. Aly Ex'r.

O. I. No. *1,123,871*

Christian O. Morbeck

Co. *H.*, *15* Reg't *Wis. Vol. Inf't.*

Department of the Interior,

BUREAU OF PENSIONS

SEP 16 1898

RECEIVED

Washington, D. C.,

Sir:

Will you kindly answer, at your earliest convenience, the questions enumerated below? The information is requested for future use, and it may be of great value to your family.

Very respectfully,

Mr. Christian O. Morbeck,

Ingalls,

Mich.

Commissioner.

No. 1. Are you a married man? If so, please state your wife's full name, and her maiden name.

Answer: *Yes — Constance C (Anderson)*

No. 2. When, where, and by whom were you married? Answer: *Mar 11th 1875*
W Green Bay Wis by Rev A M Iverson

No. 3. What record of marriage exists? Answer: *Can be found in the Records of the Moravian Church — W. Green Bay*

No. 4. Were you previously married? If so, please state the name of your former wife and the date and place of her death or divorce. Answer: *No*

No. 5. Have you any children living? If so, please state their names and the dates of their birth. Answer: *Yes,* *Arthur C Morbeck* born *Mar 9th 1879*
Clara E Morbeck born *Mar 29th 1881*
George C. " *Nov 8th 1883.*
March J. " *Mar 17th 1886*
James Garfield " *Oct 8th 1890*
Birdie Constance " *Mar 19th 1894*

Date of reply, *Sept 12th*, 1898

Christian O Morbeck
(Signature.)

0-2

Christian O. Morbeck. Pension File (Corporal Co. F, 15th Regiment Wisconsin Infantry) *Washington, D.C.: National Archives.*

Locating Union and Confederate Records

(3—148.)

INDEX
TO SPECIAL EXAMINER'S REPORT.

Claim of *Samuel Harrop*   No. 522685

PAGES.	NAMES OF WITNESSES, ETC.	Exhibits.	Deposi-tions.	REPUTATION.
1 to	Index			
	Notice to claimant *Served*			
3 to 6	Summary			
to	Claimant's statement			
7–10	Mrs. Mary Harrop	A		Excellent
11–14	John Sufton	B		Good. See 12 B.J.
15	Harriet Page	C		Good
17–18	Joseph F. Martin	D		Good.
19–20	Chas. A. Hill	E		Good.
21–22	John Walker	F		Good
23–24	Geo. W. Caraway	G		Good.
25–26	James Mullineaux	H		Excellent
27–28	Mrs. Philena Mullineaux	I		Excellent.
29–30	Andrew W. Langley	J		Good.
31–32	E. Wisdale	K		Good.
33–34	S. S. Pritchett	L		Good.
35	J. C. Priester	M		Excellent

Samuel Harrop. Pension File (Corporal 91st Ohio Infantry, Company B) Washington, D.C.:National Archives. The reason to request other pages in the Pension File–notice the list of informative affidavits contained in the file.

DEPOSITION A

Case of *Samuel Harrop*, No. 522 685

On this 10th day of March, 1888, at Gallipolis, County of Gallia State of Ohio, before me, J. G. Downtain, a Special Examiner of the Pension Office, personally appeared Mary Harrop, who, being by me first duly sworn to answer truly all interrogatories propounded to her, during this Special Examination of aforesaid pension claim, deposes and says: I am 78 years old. Residence and P.O. address as above. I am the widow of her James Harrop, and the mother of claimant Samuel, was twenty years old when he enlisted. He had hardly ever taken a dose of medicine up to that time, and I believe he was the stoutest of my four sons of which he was the oldest but one. He came home once while the regiment was still at Point Pleasant W.Va four miles above here, but that was only a few weeks after he enlisted. That was the last time I saw him until he was brought home from hospital in the early part of 1865. My son-in-law, Mr. Joseph Morrison, a shoe merchant of Mason City, Iowa, went after him and brought him home. He was in a terrible condition, almost unable to talk to us; his flesh was blue and he had dropsy, his feet being so terribly swollen that he was unable to wear his shoes. I did not observe any difficulty with his mouth except his tongue. His teeth became loose and one of them came out before he got well. He had a hole in his hip you could have put a silver dollar in. I could not particularly say whether there was any difficulty of the throat, lungs, or heart. He was not able to talk much, and tell us what was the matter with him. He had no diarrh when he came home, and I did not hear him complain much of rheumatism in his

Page 7 Deposition A

(1022—100 M.) 6—288

Samuel Harrop. Pension File (Corporal 91st Ohio Infantry, Company B) *Washington, D.C.:National Archives. The reason to request other pages in the Pension File–affidavit written by his mother about her "Sammy".*

Locating Union and Confederate Records

REMARRIED WIDOW.	(3-H-9)
NAME OF CLAIMANT: Abbott, Caroline L.	
NAME OF SOLDIER: Paddock, Theodore A.	
SERVICE: G 18 Mass. Inf.	
NUMBER: ORIG.	CTF. 31,173
DATE OF FILING: Nov 15 1901	
REMARKS:	

REMARRIED WIDOW.	
NAME OF CLAIMANT: Abbott, Ellen M.	
NAME OF SOLDIER: Morse, Henry N.	
SERVICE: F 6. Minn. Inf.	
NUMBER: ORIG. 1150725 CTF.	
DATE OF FILING: Dec 3? 19??	
REMARKS:	

REMARRIED WIDOW.	(3-H-9)
NAME OF CLAIMANT: Abbott, Clara M.	
NAME OF SOLDIER: Mills, Palemon C.	
SERVICE: B 33 Mass. Inf.	
NUMBER: ORIG. CTF. 767,733	
DATE OF FILING: July 19, 1920.	
REMARKS:	

REMARRIED WIDOW.	(3
NAME OF CLAIMANT: Abbott, Frances G.	
NAME OF SOLDIER: Bonham, Francis P.	
SERVICE: L 2 Ga. Inf.	
NUMBER: ORIG. 1669989 CTF.	
DATE OF FILING:	
REMARKS: Act of May 1, 1926	

REMARRIED WIDOW.	(8-11-9)
NAME OF CLAIMANT: Abbott Elizabeth	
NAME OF SOLDIER: Abbott, William J.	
SERVICE: I 173 N.Y. Inf.	
NUMBER: ORIG. CTF. 437751	
DATE OF FILING: Dec 20, 1917	
REMARKS:	

REMARRIED WIDOW.	(3
NAME OF CLAIMANT: Abbott, Hattie J.	
NAME OF SOLDIER: Griswold, Theodore L.	
SERVICE: F 39 Wis. Inf.	
NUMBER: ORIG. CTF. 3226	
DATE OF FILING: Sept. 13, 1920	
REMARKS: ACT OF MAY 1, 19?	

REMARRIED WIDOW.	(3-H-9)
NAME OF CLAIMANT: Abbott, Ella M.	
NAME OF SOLDIER: Lockhard, Lemira W.	
SERVICE: K 44 U.S. Col. Inf.	
NUMBER: ORIG. 1723648	
DATE OF FILING: Aug 19, 1932	
REMARKS: Act of ?	

REMARRIED WIDOW.	
NAME OF CLAIMANT: Abbott, Huldah C.	
NAME OF SOLDIER: Hopkins, Wellington H.	
SERVICE: D 7 Ohio Cav.	
NUMBER: ORIG. CTF. ?660?	
DATE OF FILING: July 31, 1926	
REMARKS:	

Index to Pension Application Files of Remarried Widows Based on Service in
Civil War and Later Wars and in the Regular Army
after the Civil War. *National Archives Microcopy M1785.*
Washington, D.C.: National Archives.

GILLILAND (continued) McClaren of Co A 6th OH Cav

Lovina C., WC-103251 filed 18 Dec 1909, widow of John Sutley of Cos B & I 39th PA Inf

Margaret A., WC-911154 filed 3 Dec 1930, widow of Francis T. Gilliland of Co B 192nd OH Inf

GILLIS, Ellen M., WC-313210 filed 19 Dec 1908 & 4 Oct 1916 also see IO-389945, widow of William H. Tonkin of Co I 9th NJ Inf, also see Mex War claim SC-6303 for George A. Gillis

Mary J.E., WC-639559 filed 12 Apr 1928, widow of Leroy W. Rodgers of Co D 98th OH Inf

Mary S., WO-1617541 filed 20 Jun 1928, widow of Ernest L. Sprague of Co C 1st ME Hvy Arty

Nancy C., WO-764564 filed 17 May 1917, widow of Alexander T. Rodgers alias William A. Rodgers of Co B 12th TN Cav

Sarah H., WC-174194 filed 25 Nov 1916, widow of William Woodburn Scott of Co I 77th OH Inf

105th OH Inf

Laura F., WO-1608323 filed 17 Mar 1928, widow of Christopher Jackson of Co K 2nd AL Inf

Lavinia B., WC-669635 filed 11 Feb 1925, widow of James M. Tar of Co D 8th MA Inf & Co C 3rd MA Cav

Lucretia, WO-859343 filed 19 Jun 1924, widow of James I. Gilmore of A 156th OH Inf

Martha, WO-533238 & WC-821322 filed 18 Sep 1916 & 1 Dec 1924 see CO-574453, widow of Joseph Heil of Co I 24th IA Inf

Mary C., Old War F-29311 & C-1811 filed 18 Oct 1851, widow Lemons Abney a Pvt in Co D of the SC Vols in the Mex War

Mary E., WC-349375 filed 14 May 1901, widow of William A. Porte Co A 80th OH Inf

Nina E., WO-939606 filed 11 Sep 1930, widow of Harry M. Thum Thurna (not clearly written) of Co B 4th MO Inf

SusanM., WC-32287 filed 30 Oct 1916 also see MC-106798, widov

Major, 130	William H. H., 302	Totten
Toles	**Tongue**	Alfred E., 208
Samuel H., 450	Evander E., 724	Joseph G., 462
Tolhurst	Levi L., 141	Recy, 725
David, 678	**Tonkin**	**Tottersman**
Toliver	William H., 270	John W., 256
Christopher, 592	**Tonne**	**Touchton**
Frank, 368	Julius H., 724	William, 44
John H., 413	**Tonorio**	**Tourile**
Tolle	Jose Ma, 724	Thomas, 266
Francis H., 566	**Tonsnel**	**Tourtellotte**
George H., 314	Charles J., 114	Alfred, 721
James M., 686	**Toohey**	**Tourtillotte**
Tolliver	Annie, 436	Arthur D., 349
John H., 214	**Tooker**	**Tousley**
John T., 716	William, 674	Henry, 8
Tolman	Wm. H., 369	Theodore, 386

A great source to help locate the remarried widows of Union soldiers is Virgil D. White's *Index to US Military Pension Applications of Remarried Widows for Service Between 1812 and 1911*. (Waynesboro, Tennessee: The National Historical Publishing Company, 1999). This index is particularly useful if you do not know the widow's new surname.

Ruffin, Pvt. Edmund, Confederate soldier. Ruffin is credited
with having fired the first shot against Fort Sumter.
National Archives and Records Administration

14

Confederate Pension Records

Pensions were granted to Confederate veterans, widows, and orphans by the former Confederate states through state funds. The pension files may include information on a soldier's military service, family members, places of residence and other genealogical data. Addresses below are the repositories for Confederate pension records. The veteran or his widow was eligible to apply for a pension to the *State in which he lived*, even if he served in a unit from a different State. Generally, an applicant was eligible for a pension only if he was indigent or disabled. The Family History Library has many of the states' pension records available which are also available through their microfilm rental program to a Family History Center near your home. Information is for the first year of eligibility for each category. This information is *not* available through the National Archives.

STATE	Veteran	Disabled Veteran	Widow	FHL Microfilm #
Alabama Dept of Archives and History 624 Washington Ave Montgomery, AL 36130-0100 (334) 242-4435	1891	1867	1886	1533719 (starting number)
Arkansas History Commission and State Archives 1 Capitol Mall Little Rock, AR 72201 (501) 682-6900	1891		1915 & mothers	1722443-1722563
Florida State Archives 500 South Bronough Street Tallahassee, FL 32399-0250 (850) 245-6700	1885		1889	0006717-006885 by file nos. Index is first roll
Georgia Dept of Archives and History 330 Capitol Ave. SE Atlanta, GA 30334 (404) 656-2817	1894	1870, 1879	1879	315678 (starting number)
Kentucky Dept. for Libraries and Archives Research Room 300 Coffee Tree Road Frankfort, KY 40602-0537 (502) 564-5773	1912	1912	1912	1670795-1670844
Louisiana State Archives 3951 Essen Lane Baton Rouge, LA 70809-2137 (225) 922-1000	1898	1898	1898	1704156 item 17
Mississippi Dept of Archives and History P.O. Box 571 Jackson, MS 39205-0571 (601) 359-6975	1888	1888	1888	902556 (starting number)

Missouri State Archives 600 W. Main P.O. Box 1747 Jefferson City, MO 65102 (573) 751-3280	1911	1911		1021101- 1021127
North Carolina Division of Archives and History 109 East Jones Street Raleigh, NC 27601-2807 (919) 733-7305		1867 & 1885		175779 Index (starting number)
Oklahoma Department of Libraries Archives and Records Management Division 200 Northeast 18th Street Oklahoma City, OK 73105-3298 (405) 522-3562	1915	1915	1915	1001529- 1001548
South Carolina Dept of Archives and History 8301 Parkland Road Columbia, SC 29223 (803) 896-6100	1887	1887	1887	
Tennessee State Library and Archives Public Service Division 403 Seventh Avenue North Nashville, TN 37243-0312 (615) 741-2764	1891		1905	978497 (starting number)
Texas State Library and Archives Commission P.O. Box 12927 Austin, TX 78711 (512) 463-5480	1889	1881 land	1889	960279 (starting number)
Library of Virginia Archives Division 800 East Broad Street Richmond, VA 23219-1905 (804) 692-3888	1888		1888	1439763 (starting number)

Best Bet for Tennessee

Family Tree Maker Family Archive #155, Military Records: Civil War Confederate Pension Applications Index. This CD contains the images of the pages of Samuel Sistler's book, Tennessee Confederate Pension Applications Index as well as an alphabetical name index. Access to approximately 28,000 individuals who applied for Civil War Confederate pensions in Tennessee. Applicant was either a Confederate soldier or a deceased soldier's widow.

Civil War Questionnaires done by Tennessee Historical Committee in 1914, 1915, and 1920, mailed to all Civil War Veterans in the state. About 1,600 questionnaires were returned. Family History Library has the index as well as the questionnaires on microfilm. The Family History Library microfilm rolls are numbered 975591 - 975599.

SOLDIER'S APPLICATION FOR PENSION.

STATE OF NORTH CAROLINA,

COUNTY OF _Burke_

On this _1_ day of _July_, A. D. 190_7_, personally appeared before me,
_____, C. S. C. in and for the State and County aforesaid,
W. A. Hildebrand, age _63_ years, and a resident at
Connelly Springs, N. C. post-office in said County and State, and who, being duly sworn,
makes the following declaration in order to obtain the pension under the provision of an act entitled
"An act for the relief of certain Confederate Soldiers, Sailors and Widows," ratified March 8, 1907;
that he is the identical _W. A. Hildebrand_
_____ who enlisted in Co. _E_, _16_ Reg. N. C. State Troops,
on or about the _10_ day of _May_ 186_1_, to serve in the armies
of the late Confederate States, and that while in said service at _____,
in the State of _____, on or about the ___ day of _____,
186__, he received a wound or wounds, etc.

(Applicant will here state the nature and extent of his wounds and disability, so that a proper classification can be made under the new Pension Law passed by the General Assembly of 1907. Read said section of said law carefully, and to accomplish the classification therein called for, let statement here as to nature and extent of wounds, disability, etc., be very full and explicit).

_I enlisted in the beginning of the War
& served all through the War, and
from this exposure I am growing weak
& can not do as much as a half days
work each day & not able to do that
I am greatly disabled from manual labor_

He further states that he is, and has been for twelve months immediately preceding this Application for Pension, a *bona fide* resident of North Carolina; that he holds no office under the United States, or under any State or County, for which he is receiving the sum of three hundred dollars as fees or as salary annually; that he is not worth in his own right, or the right of his wife, property at its assessed value for taxation to the amount of five hundred dollars ($500), nor has he disposed of property of such value by gift or voluntary conveyance since the 11th of March, 1885, and that he is not receiving any aid from the State of North Carolina or under any other statute providing for the relief of the maimed and blind soldiers of the State.

Sworn and subscribed to before me, this

day of_____, 190__   _W. A. Hildebrand_
_____   Signature of Applicant.
Signature of C. S. C.

Also personally appeared before me _J. C. Hall_, who
resides at _McGalver_ post-office, in said County and State, a person whom
I know to be respectable and entitled to credit and being by me duly sworn, says he is acquainted with
W. A. Hildebrand, the applicant for pension, and has every reason to
believe that he is the identical person he represents himself to be, and that the facts set forth in this
affidavit are correct to the best of his knowledge and belief, and that he has no interest, direct or indirect, in this claim.

Sworn and subscribed to before me, this_____

W. A. Hildebrand
Co E – 16 –
died July 11 – 1935

WIDOW'S APPLICATION FOR CONFEDERATE PENSION

STATE OF NORTH CAROLINA

COUNTY OF _Burke_

TO THE NORTH CAROLINA CONFEDERATE PENSION BOARD:

I herewith make application to the State of North Carolina, for a Confederate Pension, under the general pension laws of the State, as amended by the regular session of the General Assembly of _927:

My Name _E. C. Hildebra____ Age _50_

Residence _Conley Springs R. F. D. #_

My Late Husband's Name _W. A. Hildebran____

My husband's record in Confederate Army:

Date Enlisted _not sure_ Where Enlisted? _Morganton_

Company _C._ , Regiment _16th_ . N. C. S. T.

Was your late husband a deserter? _no_

When did you marry him? _about 1875_

When did he die? _July 11 – 1935_

Did he draw a pension before his death? _yes_ When? _June_ Where? _Morganton_

Are you now a widow? _yes_

Are you now an inmate of a State-supported Home, or Hospital, or Asylum, or County Home? _no_

Are you now receiving a pension from any other State or from the United States Government? _no_

Are you now holding a National, State, or County Office or position which pays annually in salary or fees

the sum of $300.00? _no_

Are you now receiving aid from the State under any act, general or special, providing for the relief of

soldiers or widows who are blind or maimed? _no_

Do you own property whose tax valuation exceeds $2,000.00? _no_

If so, state amount _____

Pension file: W.A. Hildebrand, Company E, 16th Regiment, N.C.S.T. *Confederate Pension Records. North Carolina Department of Cultural Resources, Department of Archives and History.*

THE STATE OF TEXAS, }
COUNTY OF _Montague_ }

To the Honorable County Judge of _Montague_ *County, Texas.*

Your petitioner, Mrs. _Mary J. Harwell_ respectfully represents that she is a resident citizen of _Montague_ County, in the State of Texas; that she is the widow of _Richard J. Harwell_ deceased, who was a Confederate soldier (or sailor), and that she makes this application for the purpose of obtaining a pension as the widow of said _Richard J. Harwell_ deceased, under the act passed by the Twenty-sixth Legislature of the State of Texas, and approved May 12, A. D. 1899, the same being an act entitled "An act to carry into effect the amendment to the Constitution of the State of Texas, providing that aid may be granted to disabled and dependent Confederate soldiers, sailors, and their widows under certain conditions, and to make an appropriation therefor," and I do solemnly swear that the answers I have given to the following questions are true.

NOTE—Applicant must make answer to all of the following questions, and such answers must be written out plainly in ink.

Q. What is your name? Answer _Mrs Mary J. Harwell_

Q. What is your age? Answer _Seventy five_

Q. In what County do you reside? Answer _Montague_

Q. How long have you resided in said County and what is your post office address? Answer _24 years Nocona Texas_

Q. Have you applied for a pension under the Confederate Pension Law heretofore, and been rejected? If so, state when and where. Answer _No_

Q. What is your occupation if able to engage in one? Answer _Not able to engage in_

Q. What is your physical condition? Answer _Very feeble_

Q. What was the name of your deceased husband? Answer _Richard J. Harwell_

Q. Were you married to him anterior to March 1, 1866? If so, on what date were you married to him and where? Answer _Yes 1860 Bulloch Co. Ala_

Q. What was the date of his death? Answer _Jan 31 1903_

Q. Are you unmarried, and have you so remained unmarried since the death of your said husband for whose services you claim a pension? Answer _Yes_

Q. In what State was your husband's command originally organized? Answer _Ala_

Q. How long did your husband serve? Give date of enlistment and discharge. Answer _Reference is hereby made to proof of R J Harwell's certificate in Comptroller ?_

Q. What was the name or letter of your husband's company and name or number of his regiment? Answer _reference is hereby made to proof of Richard J Harwell's Certificate in Comptrollers office_

Q. State whether he served in the infantry, artillery, cavalry, or the navy. Answer _Same reference as above_

Q. State whether or not you have received any pension or veteran donation land certificate under any previous law, and if you answer in the affirmative state what pension or veteran donation land certificate you have received. Answer _No_

Confederate Pension Records. Texas State Library and Archives Commission. Pension File: Mary J. Harwell, widow of Richard J. Harwell, Dawson's Cavalry Rangers.

Portrait of Pvt. Joph White, drummer boy, Virginia Regiment, C.S.A. *Library of Congress, Prints & Photographs Division. Copy photo made by LC in 1961 of ambrotype in collection of Worth Bailey, Alexandria, Va. (LC-B8184-10297)*

15

Confederate Amnesty Papers

Pardon Petitions in Response to President Andrew Johnson's Amnesty Proclamations of May 29, 1865 (National Archives M1003)

This record contains applications for pardon, 1865-1867, submitted to President Andrew Johnson by former Confederates excluded from the provisions of his amnesty proclamation of May 29, 1865, together with affidavits, oaths of allegiance, and other accompanying papers. A presidential pardon would restore a citizen to his former civil rights and provide immunity from prosecution for treason and confiscation of property. The oaths vary in content from the minimum of the single document of the loyalty oath, to the oath plus other agreements to accept conditions of the pardon.

Loyalty Oaths, or pardon applications, were taken by former Confederates and provided the following: *name of person, county of residence, number of months of residence in the state, the exact birth date, generally the county and state of birth, and naturalization date and place.* Approximately 15,000 applications were filed, primarily by propertied persons who were anxious to gain pardon to prevent possible confiscation of property and finances, and the suspension of their voting rights.

It is best to use the Name Index to files first.

Locating Union and Confederate Records

STATE	NATIONAL ARCHIVES # *	FHL MICROFILM #
Name Index to Files	M1003 roll 1	1578739
Alabama	M1003 rolls 1-12	1578740 - 1578750
Arkansas	M1003 rolls 13-14	1578751 - 1578752
California	M1003 roll 73	1587811
Delaware	M1003 roll 73	1587811
District of Columbia	M1003 roll 73	1587811
Florida	M1003 roll 15	1578753
Georgia	M1003 rolls 16-24	1578754 - 1578762
Illinois	M1003 roll 73	1587811
Indiana	M1003 roll 73	1587811
Iowa	M1003 roll 73	1587811
Kansas	M1003 roll 73	1587811
Kentucky	M1003 rolls 25-26	1578763 - 1578764
Louisiana	M1003 rolls 27-29	1578765 - 1578767
Maryland	M1003 roll 30	1578768
Massachusetts	M1003 roll 73	1587811
Michigan	M1003 roll 73	1587811
Mississippi	M1003 rolls 31-35	1578769 - 1578773
Missouri	M1003 roll 36	1578774
Nebraska	M1003 roll 73	1587811
New Jersey	M1003 roll 73	1587811
New Mexico Terr.	M1003 roll 73	1587811
New York	M1003 roll 73	1587811
North Carolina	M1003 rolls 37-43	1578775 - 1578781
Ohio	M1003 roll 73	1587811
Pennsylvania	M1003 roll 73	1587811
Rhode Island	M1003 roll 73	1587811
South Carolina	M1003 rolls 44-47	1578782 - 1578785
Tennessee	M1003 rolls 48-51	1578786 - 1578789
Texas	M1003 rolls 52-55	1578790 - 1578793
Virginia	M1003 rolls 56-71	1578794 - 1578809
West Virginia	M1003 roll 72	1578810
Undesignated state or Territory	M1003 roll 73	1587811

*To order HeritageQuest films in Series M1003 see chapter 22.

Book

Pardons by the President: Final Report of the Names of Persons Who Lived in Alabama, Virginia, West Virginia, or Georgia, Were Engaged in the Rebellion and Pardoned by the President, Andrew Johnson. Bowie, MD: Heritage Books, 1986.

Sample of an Amnesty Oath issued to John Buchanan. Index to Pardon Petitions in Response to President Johnson's Amnesty Proclamations of May 19, 1865. *National Archives M1003, microfilm no. 1578740, frame 272, Family History Library, Salt Lake City, Utah.*

State of Alabama } To the President of
County of Barbour } the United States,

Your Petitioner William A. Bray
a citizen of the County & State aforesaid
a Merchant by profession, has taken
the Oath of amnesty prescribed in your
proclamation, of the 29th of May. offering
pardon for offences committed against
the United States, in the late rebellion, and
asks for Special pardon. on the ground that
his property may be worth over Twenty Thou-
sand Dollars, that being the only ground
upon which he is excepted from pardon, in
said proclamation,

1st Your petitioner participated in
said rebellion, by sympathizing with it. and
serving in its armies, in the capacity of
Lieutenant.

2nd I did not order, aid in, or advise
the taking of Fort Morgan, or Mount Vernon
arsenal,

3d I have not served on any vig-
ilance Committee during the war,

4th No person has been shot or
hung by my order, for real or supposed
disloyalty to the Confederate States,

5th I have not shot or hung or
aided in shooting or hanging, any person
for real or supposed disloyalty to the
Confederate States,

6th I have not ordered or been
engaged in hunting any one with dogs
who was disloyal to the Confederate
States an supposed to be,

Index to Pardon Petitions in Response to President Johnson's Amnesty
Proclamations of May 19, 1865. *National Archives M1003, microfilm no.
1578740, Family History Library, Salt Lake City, Utah.*

7th. I was in favor of the so called Ordinance of Secession, at the time it was passed.

I will be a peaceable, loyal citizen of the United States for the future,

I have received no notice to show cause why my property Should not be Confiscated,

No property belonging to me is in the possession of the United States, as abandoned property or otherwise,

My Oath of Amnesty is hereunto attached,

Wm. H. Bray

Sworn to and Subscribed before me this 7th Nov. 1865
J Beeman Notary Public
Barbour County Ala.

United States of America
State of Alabama Barbour County
I, William H C Bray of said State & County, do Solemnly Swear in presence of Almighty God, That I will henceforth faithfully Support and defend the Constitution of the United States and the Union of the States thereunder and that I will in like manner abide by and faithfully Support all laws and proclamations which have been made during the existing rebellion in reference to the emancipation of Slaves So help me God,
Sworn to and Subscribed before me this Nov. 7th. 1865
J Beeman Notary Public
Barbour County Al—

Wm H Bray

Amnesty Oath of William H. Bray, Pardon Petitions to
President Johnson's Amnesty Proclamations of May 19, 1865.
National Archives M1003, microfilm no. 1578740,
Family History Library, Salt Lake City, Utah.

Locating Union and Confederate Records

Confederate Amnesty Papers Index

Bryce, Campbell R. (S. C.)
Bryson, James (Miss.)
Bryson, Tadders D. (N. C.)
Buchanan, John (Ala.)
Buchanan, John R. (Md.)
Buchanan, Richard (Ala.)
Buchanan, Thomas J. (Miss.)
Buchannon, James (Ga.)
Bunchanon, Benjamin K. (Va.)
Bunchanon, James S. (Va.)
Buck, Isaac N. (Va.)
Buck, James (Miss.)
Buck, James Q. (Miss.)

Bunkley, James (Ga.)
Bunting, Thomas (N. C.)
Burbidge, John W. (S. C.)
Burbridge, John (Mo.)
Burch, George H. (Va.)
Burch, Marion M. (Ky.)
Burch, R. E. (N. C.)
Burdett, Thomas P. (Ga.)
Burdine, John W. (Va.)
Burene, Absolom L. (Tenn.)
Burge, Wiley T. (S. C.)
Burge, William T. (Ga.)
Burgess, James M. (N. C.)

Index to Pardon Petitions in Response to President Johnson's Amnesty Proclamations of May 19, 1865. *National Archives M1003, microfilm no. 1578739, Family History Library, Salt Lake City, Utah.*

Washington, D.C. Convalescent soldiers and others outside quarters of the Sanitary Commission Home Lodge. *Library of Congress, Prints & Photographs Division (LC-B817-7716)*

16

Soldiers' Homes

National Homes for Disabled Volunteer Soldiers

Established in Congress in 1866 for needy veterans of the army, marines, and organized militia called into federal service, the National Homes were to provide for those disabled by disease or wounds and without adequate means of support. After 1930 these homes became known as Veterans Administration Homes. Registers of residents for most of the homes are available at the National Archives and through the Family History Library. These include registers of death and hospitalization. Branch homes were founded in the following cities in the years shown.

RECORDS OF NATIONAL HOMES FOR DISABLED VOLUNTEER SOLDIERS 1866-1937, NATIONAL ARCHIVES P2260

STATE	FAMILY HISTORY LIBRARY MICROFILM #
California	1577617 (starting number)
Illinois	1548682 (starting number)
Indiana	1571582 (starting number)
Kansas	1578738 (starting number)
Maine	1549002 (starting number)
New York	1536167 (starting number)
Ohio	1547608 (starting number)
Oregon	1578117 (starting number)
South Dakota	1547492 (starting number)
Tennessee	1571745 (starting number)
Virginia	1578118 (starting number)
Wisconsin	1561060 (starting number)

Locating Union and Confederate Records

APPLICATION FOR ADMISSION

——TO THE——

CONFEDERATE SOLDIERS' HOME

AT HIGGINSVILLE, MISSOURI

OFFICERS OF THE HOME.

)R. W. A. WEBB, Surgeon.   COL. GEORGE P. GROSS, Superintendent.   CAPT. R. H. BENTON, Assistant Superintendent.

BOARD OF MANAGERS.

P. H. FRANKLIN, President, Marshall, Mo.   B. F. MURDOCK, Vice-President, Platte City, Mo.   JOHN A. WOODS, Secretary, Fayette, Mo.

J. D. INGRAM, Treasurer, Nevada, Mo.   J. W. HALLIBURTON, Carthage, Mo.

STATE OF MISSOURI,

County of Randolph, ss

I, Thomas Alonzo Haggard

ereby apply for admission to the Confederate Soldiers' Home of Missouri. My full name is............

Thomas Alonzo Haggard

was born on the 10 day of Oct, 1849, at Monroe County, Miss

y present residence is Huntsville, Randolph Co.

y postoffice address is Huntsville, County of Randolph, State of Missouri.

have lived continuously in the State of Missouri for 65 years immediately preceding this

oplication.

enlisted in the Confederate Army, at the town of Lexington, date October, 1864 in the County of ....

the State of Missouri in Capt Frank Haire Company, Col Perkins Regiment, Price

rigade. My rank was private. I was engaged in the following battles

"Big Blue" three or four others that I can't call to mind

ever wounded, state when and where "no."

ever captured, state when and where Captured near Joplin

ever in prison, state when and where Rock Island Prison 6 mts 2 da

ate when paroled or discharged Released at the close of the war.

Confederate Soldiers' Home Application, Missouri. *Family History Library, microfilm no. 1021107, Salt Lake City, Utah.*

Soldiers' Homes

RECORDS AVAILABLE THROUGH THE FAMILY HISTORY LIBRARY CATALOG FOR STATES WITH CONFEDERATE HOMES:

STATE	FAMILY HISTORY LIBRARY MICROFILM #
Missouri	1021101 - 1021127
Tennessee	969840 - 969842
Texas	960664 (starting number)

RECORDS AVAILABLE THROUGH THE FAMILY HISTORY LIBRARY CATALOG FOR STATES WITH UNION SOLDIERS' HOMES:

STATE	FAMILY HISTORY LIBRARY MICROFILM #
Michigan	925040 (starting number)
Ohio	928927 (starting number)

Registers of residents, hospital admissions, deaths lists, and related records are available at each of these homes or at the state archives.

California	National Home for Soldiers (Federal)—Santa Monica (LA)
	Veteran's Home of California—Yountville, Napa County
	Women's Relief Corps Home—San Jose
Colorado	Soldiers' and Sailors' Home
Connecticut	Fitch's Home for Soldiers—Darien Heights
District of Columbia	Soldiers' and Sailors' Temporary Home
	U.S. Soldiers & Airmen Home (Federal)
Idaho	Soldiers' Home—Boise
Illinois	National Home for Soldiers (Federal)—Danville
	Soldiers' and Sailors' Home—Quincy
	Soldiers' Widows' Home—Wilmington
Indiana	National Home for Soldiers (Federal)—Marion
	Soldiers' Home—Lafayette

Iowa	Soldiers' Home—Marshalltown
Kansas	National Home for Soldiers (Federal)—Leavenworth
	State Soldiers' Home—Dodge
	Bickerdyke Annex—Dodge
Maine	National Home for Soldiers (Federal)—Togus
Massachusetts	National Soldiers' Home—Wollaston
	Soldiers' Home—Chelsea
Michigan	Soldiers' Home—Grand Rapids
Minnesota	Soldiers' Home—Minneapolis
Mississippi	Beauvoir Confederate Veterans Home & Cemetery—Biloxi
Missouri	Federal Soldiers' Home—St. James
	Missouri Confederate Soldiers Home & Memorial—Higginsville
Montana	Soldiers' Home—Columbia Falls
Nebraska	Soldiers' and Sailors' Home—Milford
	Soldiers' and Sailors' Home—Burkett
New Hampshire	Soldiers' Home—Tilton
New Jersey	Home for Disabled Soldiers—Arlington
	Home for Soldiers and Sailors, etc.—Vineland
New York	The National Home for Soldiers (Federal), (formerly New York State Soldiers' and Sailors' Home, est. 1877)—Bath
	Sailors' Snug Harbor—New Brighton
	Woman's Relief Corps Home—Oxford
North Carolina	North Carolina Confederate Soldiers Home (White veterans)—Raleigh
	North Carolina Confederate Soldiers Home (Black veterans)—Goldsboro
North Dakota	Soldiers' Home—Lisbon
Ohio	The Madison Home—Madison
	National Home for Soldiers (Federal)—Dayton
	State Soldiers' Home—Erie County
Oklahoma	Union Soldiers' Home—Oklahoma City
	Confederate Soldiers' Home—Ardmore
Oregon	Soldiers' Home—Roseburg
Pennsylvania	Soldiers' and Sailors' Home—Erie
	Memorial Home—Brockville

	Home for Veterans and Wives—Philadelphia U.S. Naval Home (Federal)—Philadelphia
Rhode Island	Soldiers' Home—Bristol
South Dakota	Battle Mountain Sanatarium—Hot Springs
Tennessee	The National Home for Soldiers (Federal)—Johnson City Tennessee Confederate Soldier's Home—Hermitage Plantation, Nashville
Texas	Texas Confederate Home—Austin
Vermont	Soldiers' Home—Bennington
Virginia	The National Home for Soldiers (Federal)—Hampton
Washington	Soldiers' Home—Orting Veterans' Home—Retsil (near Orchard)
Wisconsin	The National Home for Soldiers (Federal)—Milwaukee Wisconsin Veterans' Home—Waupaca County
Wyoming	Soldiers' and Sailors' Home—Buffalo

Henry Q. Taylor.

MILITARY HISTORY.

Time and Place of each Enlistment.	Rank.	Company and Regiment, or Vessel.	Time and Place of Discharge.	Cause of Discharge.	Rate of Pension.	Disability.	Read of Write.
April 16, 1861,	Priv.	A. 22 Regt. O.U.S.	Aug. 19, 1861, Athens, O.	Expiration of Service.	$12.	General.	Yes
Sept. 8, 1861, Millicothe, O.	Corp.	B. 26 Regt. O.U.S.	Oct. 21, 1865, Victoria, Tex.	Close of War.			

DOMESTIC HISTORY.

Where and when Born.	Religious Belief.	Height.	Complexion.	Color of Eyes.	Color of Hair.	OCCUPATION.	Residence Subsequent to Discharge.	What Family Living.	Name and P. O. Address of Nearest Relative.
Charlotte, Iowa April 3, 1841.	Methodist	5 ft 6	Dark.	Hazel.	Brown.	Blacksmith.	Chillicothe, Ross Co. O.	None.	Mrs. Mary E. Smith, Boycville, Dunn Co. Wis. (Sister).

HOME HISTORY.

Cottage.	Date of Admission and Re-Admission.	Appointments.	Date of Discharge.	Cause of Discharge.	Date of Death.	Cause of Death.
2.	May 17, 1890.				Nov. 30, 1898.	Arterica

GENERAL REMARKS.

PAPERS.

Admission Paper, No 1009.

3 Army Discharge,

Certificate of Service,

Pension Certificate, No 640820

EFFECTS.

Labor Money,	$	
Pension Money,	$150.50	
Personal, Appraised at $	Sold for $ ____	
Total,	$	

How Disposed of, 1 Valice & 1 cheap Watch - all delivered to A. B. Fisher Administrator - Sandusky O. Dec 10/98

2

John G. O'Connor B Co 69th N.Y.

MILITARY HISTORY.

Time and Place of each Enlistment.	Rank.	Company and Regiment.	Time and Place of Discharge.	Cause of Discharge.	Kind and Degree of Disability.	When and where Contracted.
Aug 11. 1861	Pvt 39	2 Batt. V. R. C	May. 4. Oct 6. 1864 Washington, D.C.	Expiration of term		
May 5. 1864	36		Sept 5. 1866 Washington, D.C.	Instructions from A G O Aug 21 1864	Rheumatism in hip	

DOMESTIC HISTORY. Catholic

WHERE BORN.	Age.	Height.	Complexion.	Color of Eyes.	Color of Hair.	OCCUPATION.	Residence Subsequent to Discharge.	Married or Single.	P. O. Address of Nearest Relative.
Ireland	40	5.6	sandy	grey	brown	Laborer	Boston, Mass	single	

HOME HISTORY.

Rate of Pension	Date of Admission and Re-Admission.	Condition of Re-Admission.	Date of Discharge.	Cause of Discharge.	Date of Death.	Cause of Death.
8	Adm E.B. June 3/69 Read N.E.B. Dec 11. 71 Trans P.B. Aug 10. 88		Jan 31. 1870		Aug 10. 03	Exhaustion

GENERAL REMARKS.

PAPERS.

Admission Paper,   1

Army Discharge,   2

Certificate of Service,

Pension Certificate,   1

EFFECTS.

Labor Money, Cash $ 10.00

Pension Money, $ 49.00

Personal, Appraised at $ None Sold for $

Total, $

How Disposed of

National Soldiers' Home Records, Ohio. *Family History Library,*
microfilm no. 1577623, Salt Lake City, Utah.

Washington, D.C. Noncommissioned officers of Company H, 10th Veteran Reserve Corps, at Washington Circle. *1865 April. Library of Congress, Prints & Photographs Division (LC-B8171-7802)*

17

Veteran Organizations

Grand Army of The Republic

The Grand Army of the Republic (GAR) was the Union veteran's organization. They had local post meeting, annual encampments at the state and local level. Websites of their successor organizations, the Sons of Union Veterans of the Civil War *(www.suvcw.org)* will also give a link to the women's *(www.suvcw.org/duv.htm)* and state organizations. Many records of the GAR are in the custody of state and local historical organizations or the state adjutant general. Records on the veterans can contain name, age, birthplace, occupation, residence, regiment, length of service, as well as possible personal information about their service and narratives about their most memorable war experiences. The GAR can be written directly: Grand Army of the Republic Civil War Museum and Library, Frankford Section, 4278 Griscom Street, Philadelphia, PA 19124. The addresses for the Union Veteran Organizations: Sons of Union Veterans of the Civil War, 200 Washington Street, Suite 614, Wilmington, DE 19801 and Daughters of Union Veterans of the Civil War, Library and Museum, 503 S. Walnut, Springfield, IL 62704. As the last of the Union and Confederate Veterans passed away during the 30's and 40's, the records of the veteran's organizations were often turned over to the American Legion. So check to see if the local or state American Legion has and

Grand Army of the Republic Post 41 Chelsea, Michigan. *Microfilm no. 0905734. Family History Library, Salt Lake City, Utah.*

records from the GAR or UCV. Also check local libraries and historical societies. Many of the records of the Grand Army of the Republic can be found in the Family History Library collection using an *author search* as "Grand Army of the Republic" and the information held in the Family History Library are displayed. Another method is to use the Family History Library Catalog search the Locality section under [State] - SOCIETIES.

Military Order of the Loyal Legion of the United States

This society was organized by officers of the Union Army in 1865. Their address is:

MOLLUS
1805 Pine Street
Phildadelphia, PA 19103
Telephone: 215-546-2425
Internet: suvcw.org/mollus.htm

United Confederate Veterans

This was the organization of the confederate veterans and their records may be available in the former states of the Confederacy in the custody of state and local historical organizations or in the state adjutant general office. Also check their successor organizations, the Sons of United Confederate Veterans *(www.scv.org)* and United Daughters of the Confederacy *(www.hqudc.org)*. Addresses: Sons of Confederate Veterans, Elm Springs, Box 59, Columbia, TN 38401-0059, and United Daughters of the Confederacy, P.O. Box 4868, Richmond, VA 23220. As the last of the Union and Confederate Veterans passed away during the 30's and 40's, the records of the veteran's organizations were often turned over to the American Legion. So check to see if the local or state American Legion has and records from the GAR or UCV. Also check local libraries and historical societies.

Fredericksburg, Va. Burial of soldiers. *Timothy H. O'Sullivan, 1864 May. Library of Congress, Prints & Photographs Division (LC-B8171-2509)*

18

Union
Deaths and Burials

Nearly 359,000 soldiers in the Union forces lost their lives during the war. The following book is the best source to begin searching for a Union soldier's burial place. It is also available in index form and on CD-ROM.

Roll of Honor: Names of Soldiers Who Died in Defense of the American Union. 27 volumes Washington DC: Government Printing Office, 1865-71. The Family History Library has the 27 volumes of the books available on microfilm numbers 1311589-1311591.

Ramsey, Martha and William Ramsey, compilers. *Index to the Roll of Honor*. Baltimore: Genealogical Publishing Co., 1995. (Index to the Union burials during the Civil War)

Easiest to Use

Family Tree Maker, **Family Archive CD #351**, contains the images of all 27 volumes of the Roll of Honor as well as the Unpublished Roll of Honor. It references approximately 236,000 Union soldiers who were buried in over 300 national cemeteries, garrison cemeteries, soldiers' lots, and private cemeteries. The CD gives the soldier's name, and

Soundex code, his rank, regiment, company, date of death and location of his final burial site. (This is the easiest reference to use)

Other Sources, National Archives Record Group 92

Applications for Headstones for Soldiers Buried at the Soldier's Home 1909-23.

List of Headstones for Soldiers Buried in Private Cemeteries During 1861-1882.

Registers of Superintendents at National Cemeteries, 1867-1883

Lists of Soldiers Buried in [various states and cemeteries]

Lists of Union Soldiers Buried in Various National Cemeteries 1861-79.
Arranged by state burial location and name of soldier.

Lists of Interments of Colored Troops During the Civil War.
Many lists arranged by place of burial; name cemetery or place given.

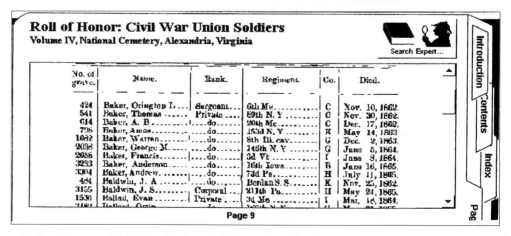

Roll of Honor: Civil War Union Soldiers. *Family Tree Maker, Family Archive CD #351, Fremont, CA: Banner Blue Software Company.*

Burial in National Cemeteries

For information concerning any of the approximately 2 million veterans interred in the 113 national cemeteries, contact the Director of Public Affairs, National Cemetery System, Department of Veterans Affairs, 810 Vermont Avenue NW, Washington, D.C. 20451.

Martha & William Reamy, Compilers. Index to the Roll of Honor. *Baltimore: Genealogical Publishing Company, 1995, 557.*

Headstone Applications

Between the years 1879 and 1925 the federal government erected headstones on the graves of Union servicemen, regardless of place of burial. The applications for these markers are arranged chronologically by state and county of burial, and there is a card index to applications filed between 1879 and 1903. Each applicant tells name, rank, military organization, date of death, cemetery of interment and its location, and name and address of applicant. The National Archives Field Branch in Alexandria, Virginia, has some later applications, including those for headstones for Confederate soldiers.

Died After the Civil War

For Veterans who died after the Civil War, check if they were granted a military pension which would give information on their death. Also the use of the US censuses and state censuses locates where he was living which can help to locate possible burial location. (see Chapter 13 for Union pension information.)

Roll for Honor: Civil War Union Soldiers. Family Tree Maker, Family Archive CD #351, Fremont, CA: Banner Blue Software Company.

Martha & William Reamy, Compilers. *Index to the Roll of Honor.* Baltimore: Genealogical Publishing Company, 1995) 557.

Richmond, Va. Graves of Confederate soldiers in Hollywood Cemetery, with
board markers. *1865. Library of Congress, Prints & Photographs Division
(LC-B8171-0931)*

19

Confederate Deaths and Burials

Some Confederate deaths have been listed in the multiple volume work, *The War of the Rebellion: A Compilation of the Official Records of the Union and Confederate Armies.* (Washington, D.C.: U.S. Government Printing Office, 1880-1900). The National Archives Film Group M836 and the Family History Library have microfilm copies. The lists and narratives are arranged alphabetically by the state and locality where the engagement occurred and then by military unit number followed by units identified by the surname of the commanding officer.

STATES	NATIONAL ARCHIVES FILM *	FHL MICROFILM #
Alabama, Arkansas, Florida, Georgia, Kentucky	M836 Roll 1	1025132
Louisiana, Maryland, Mississippi	M 836 Roll 2	1025133
Missouri, New Mexico, North Carolina, Pennsylvania, South Carolina	M 836 Roll 3	1025134
Tennessee, Texas	M 836 Roll 4	1025135
Virginia, Aldie—Fredericksburg	M 836 Roll 5	1025136
Virginia, Fredericksburg— Seven Days' Campaign	M 836 Roll 6	1025137

Virginia, Shenandoah Valley—Yorktown,
miscellaneous, West Virginia,
Single unit in more than one state,
Indiana Territory   M 836 Roll 7   1025138

*To order HeritageQuest films in Series M836 see chapter 22.

Other Possible Sources

Register of Confederate Soldiers and Citizens Who Died in Federal Prisons and Military Hospitals in the North. National Archives M918—one roll of microfilm. Family History Library Microfilm 1024456. Lists arranged alphabetically by location of the death, then by the name of the soldier. Series M918 is available from the HeritageQuest store. See chapter 22 for ordering information.

Register of Confederate Soldiers and Citizens Who Died in Federal Prisons and Military Hospitals in the North. Nacogdoches, Texas: Ericson Books, 1984.

Register of the Confederate Dead, Interred in Hollywood Cemetery, Richmond, VA. Gary, Clemmitt & Jones, Printers, 1869.

Official Confederate Gravestones are supplied by the US Government— Applications at National Archives Military Field Branch, Suitland, Maryland. Indexes to applications cover various spans of years.

Best Bet: Easiest to Use CD

Based on the earlier cited work, this is indexed by name. This is the quickest process. *Family Tree Maker's Family Archive #119: Military Records: Confederate Soldiers 1861-1865.* This CD contains the complete contents of National Archive microfilm roll number M918, *Register of Confederate Soldiers, Sailors, and Citizens Who Died in Federal Prisons and*

Head Quarters 2nd Brigade Mo. V. Troops
Camp on Frog Bayou, Ark. Mar. 17th 1862

To Maj. Genl.
S. Price
Cmdg. Mis. S.,

Sir,

In obedience to a special order issued from your Head Quarters, I have the honor to submit the following report of Killed and Wounded in 2nd Brigade Mo. Vol. Corps. at the recent action on Sugar Creek, Ark.

Vizt:

Brig. Genl. W.Y. Slack	Dangerously wounded
Lt. Col. Scott — Aid de Camp	Slightly "
E. R. Conelly	Mortally "
August Link	Do "
Francis Collett	Slightly "
J. Glenn	Severely "
W. C. Craig	Slightly
E. Dyson	Do
Henry Whaler	Do
Moses Horgan	Severely
B. B. White	Slightly
Jas. M. Young	Do
Lawson Moore	Do
Morris Johnson	Do
Anony Finnell	Do
Lieut. J. T. Davis	Do
Thos. Merriss	Killed
John Haigy	Mortally wounded
C. B. Craddock	Slightly "
Thos. Harlow	Do "

Confederate Death Records, *National Archives M836. Microfilm no. 1025132, Family History Library, Salt Lake City, Utah*

Locating Union and Confederate Records

Name	Rank	Co.	Regiment	Date of Death	Locality of Grave
			POINT LOOKOUT, MD., 39.		
Hunter, John,	Pvt.	H	26 Va.	Feb. 21, 1865.	Confederate Cemetery.
Hurce, William,	"	K	10 Ga. Inf.	Nov. 19, 1863.	" "
Hursey, G. A.,	Corp.	K	6 Ala. Inf.	Nov. 19, "	" "
Hutchinson, J. J.,	Pvt.	A	22 Va.	April 30, 1865.	" "
Hutchinson, J. L.,	"	G	5 Va.	March 31, "	" "
Hutchinson, Thos.,	"	I	26 Va.	May 31, "	" "
Hutchison, H.,	"	C	6 S. C. Cav.	Jan. 9, "	" "
Hyatt, R. A. L.,	"	E	Thomas' N. C. Legion.	Jan. 13, "	" "
Hyde, Samuel L.,	"	D	20 Miss. Inf.	Sept. 2, 1864.	" "
Hylton, Jeremiah,	"	B	42 Va. Inf.	Jan. 6, "	" "
Ingles, Geo. A.,	Pvt.	F	22 Va.	Dec. 31, 1864.	Confederate Cemetery.
Ingold, J. A.,	"	A	53 N. C. Inf.	Dec. 10, 1863.	" "
Ingram, J.,	"	C	1st Ga.	Sept. 27, 1864.	" "
Ingram, Wm.,	"	K	18 N. C. Inf.	Nov. 3, 1863.	" "
Inman, Alexander,	"	E	3 (40) N. C. Art.	March 9, 1865.	" "
Inman, J. A.,	"	G	5 Va. Cav.	Sept. 18, 1864.	" "
Insco, B. B.,	"	K	12 N. C. Inf.	Nov. 30, "	" "
Insco, Henry,	"	E	12 N. C. Inf.	Nov. 7, "	" "
Ipock, Albert,	Sgt.	D	3 (40) N. C. Art.	Feb. 18, 1865.	" "
Irick, W. M.,	Pvt.	E	5 S. C. Cav.	Jan. 29, "	" "
Irwin, G. N.,	"	E	3 Ala. Cav.	Nov. 1, 1863.	" "
Isbell, Robt. G.,	"	B	15 Ga. Inf.	Dec. 10, 1864.	" "
Isdel, J. T.,	"	C	59 Ga. Inf.	Oct. - 1863.	" "
Isham, Nathan,	"	A	Winis N. C. Battn.	Jan. 7, 1865.	" "
Isley, John,	"	F	1 N. C.	Aug. 8, 1864.	" "
Ivey, W. L.,	"	A	20 N. C. Inf.	Jan. 26, 1865.	" "
Jack, John H.,	Pvt.	K	52 Va. Inf.	March 27, 1864.	Confederate Cemetery.
Jackson, David,	"	E	60 Tenn.	Oct. - 1863.	" "
Jackson, Henry,	"	B	16 Va. Cav.	Jan. 24, 1865.	" "
Jackson, J. A.,	"	B	7 S. C. Cav.	April 24, 1864.	" "
Jackson, John H.,	"	G	22 N. C. Inf.	June 27, "	" "
Jackson, Lyndhurst,	"	E	3 Va. Cav.	June 24, 1865.	" "
Jackson, Peter,	"		Batty. B, Stiles' Ga. Art.	May 29, "	" "
Jackson, Thomas P.,	"		1 Mo. Cav.	Sept. 18, 1864.	" "
Jackson, Wm.,	"	A	14 Va. Inf.	Nov. 10, 1863.	" "
Jackson, Wm. C.,	"	F	14 Va.	Jan. 27, 1865.	" "
James, A. F.,	Corp.	B	17 Ga.	Oct. 26, 1864.	" "
James, Geo. T.,	Pvt.	H	55 Va.	June - 1865.	" "

National Archives, M918, Register of Confederate Soldiers, Sailors and Citizens who Died in Federal Prisons and Military Hospitals in the North, 1861-1865. *Family Tree Maker, CD 119 Military Records: Confederate Solders.*

Military Hospitals in the North, 1861-1865. The collection contains the names of approximately 25,000 individuals which are indexed. The following data is provided: name, rank, company, regiment, death date, location of death or burial, number and locality of grave.

For those who survived the Civil War, check for a Confederate Pension Record through his state of residence as the date of death is often stated in the Pension Record. (See Chapter 14 for information on Confederate pensions).

Petersburg, Va. Group of Company G, 114th Pennsylvania Infantry (Zouaves).
1864 August. Library of Congress, Prints & Photographs Division
(LC-B8171-7198)

20

Finding Aids

The National Archives and Regional Branches

National Archives and Records Administration
700 Pennsylvania Ave. NW
Washington, D.C. 20408
www.nara.gov
Tel: (800) 234-8861 Fax: (301) 713-6905
inquire@nara.gov

National Archives at College Park
8601 Adelphi Rd.
College Park, MD 20740-6001
Tel: (800) 234-8861

Washington National Records Center
4205 Suitland Rd.
Suitland, MD 20746-8001
Tel: (301) 457-7000 Fax: (301) 457-7117
center@suitland.nara.gov

NARA Pacific Alaska (Anchorage)
654 W 3rd Ave.
Anchorage, AK 99501-2145
www.nara.gov/regional/archorag.html
Tel: (907) 271-2441 Fax: (907) 271-2442
archives@alaska.nara.gov

NARA Central Plains (Kansas City)
2312 East Bannister Rd.
Kansas City, MO 64131-3011
www.nara.gov/regional/kansas.html
Tel: (816) 926-6920 Fax: (816) 926-6982
kansascity.archives@nara.gov

NARA Central Plains (Lee's Summit, MO)
200 Space Center Drive
Lee's Summit, MO 64064-1182
Tel: (816) 478-7089 Fax: (816) 478-7625
center@kccave.nara.gov

NARA Great Lakes (Chicago)
7358 S. Pulaski Road
Chicago, IL 60629-5898
www.nara.gov/regional/chicago.html
Tel: (773) 581-7816 Fax: (312) 353-1294
chicago.archives@nara.gov

NARA Great Lakes Region (Dayton)
3150 Springboro Rd.
Dayton, OH 45439-1883
Tel: (937) 225-2852 Fax: (937) 225-7236
center@dayton.nara.gov

NARA Mid-Atlantic (Center City, Philadelphia)
900 Market Street
Philadelphia, PA 19107-4292
www.nara.gov/regional/philarc.html
Tel: (215) 597-3000 Fax: (215) 597-2303
philadelphia.archives@nara.gov

NARA Northeast - Boston
Frederick C. Murphy Federal Center
380 Trapelo Rd.
Waltham, MA 02452-6399
www.nara.gov/regional/boston.html
Tel: (781) 647-8100 Fax: (781) 647-8460
waltham.center@nara.gov

NARA Northeast - New York City
201 Varick Street
New York, NY 10014-4811
www.nara.gov/regional/newyork.html
Tel: (212) 337-1300 Fax: (212) 337-1306
newyork.archives@nara.gov

NARA's Northeast (Pittsfield, MA)
10 Conte Drive
Pittsfield, Massachusetts 01201-8230
www.nara.gov/regional/pittsfie.html
Tel: (413) 445-6885 Fax: (413) 445-7305
archives@pittsfield.nara.gov

NARA Pacific Alaska (Seattle)
6125 Sand Point Way, NE
Seattle, WA 98115-7999
www.nara.gov/regional/seattle.html
Tel: (206) 526-6501 Fax: (206) 526-6575
seattle.archives@nara.gov

NARA Pacific - San Francisco
1000 Commodore Drive
San Bruno, CA 94066-2350
www.nara.gov/regional/sanfranc.html
Tel: (650) 876-9001 Fax: (650) 876-9233
sanbruno.archives@nara.gov

NARA Pacific - Laguna Niguel

24000 Avila Road, First Floor
Laguna Niguel, CA 92607-6719
www.nara.gov/regional/laguna.html
Tel: (949) 360-2641 Fax: (949) 360-2624
laguna.archives@nara.gov

NARA Rocky Mountain (Denver)

West 6th Ave. & Kipling St.
Building 48, Denver Federal Center
P.O. Box 25307
Denver, CO 80225-0307
www.nara.gov/regional/denver.html
Tel: (303) 236-0817 Fax: (303) 236-9297
denver.archives@nara.gov

NARA Southeast (Atlanta)

1557 St. Joseph Avenue
East Point, GA 30344-2593
www.nara.gov/regional/atlanta.html
Tel: (404) 763-7474 Fax: (404) 763-7059
atlanta.center@nara.gov

NARA Southwest (Ft. Worth)

501 West Felix Street, Building 1
P.O. Box 6216
Fort Worth, TX 76115-0216
www.nara.gov/regional/ftworth.html
Tel: (817) 334-5515 Fax: (817) 334-5511
ftworth.archives@nara.gov

Libraries & Archives for Genealogical and Civil War Research

National Archives & Records Admin
700 Pennsylvania Ave, NW
Washington, DC 20408
Forms by Internet: inquire@nara.gov
(specify form # and include your mailing address)

Family History Library
of The Church of Jesus Christ of Latter-day Saints
35 North West Temple
Salt Lake City, UT 84150
Phone: (801) 240-2331

Local Family History Center
check your local phone book under:
Church of Jesus Christ of Latter-day
Saints, Family History Center

Allen County Public Library
Historical Genealogy Dept.
900 Webster St.
Fort Wayne, IN 46802

California State Library
Sutro Branch
480 Winston Drive
San Francisco, CA 94132

Library of Congress
Humanities and Social Sciences Division
Thomas Jefferson Building, Room LJ G42
Washington, DC 20540-4660

Daughters of the American Revolution Library
1776 D St, NW
Washington DC, 20006-5392

Burton Historical Collection
Detroit Public Library
5201 Woodward Ave
Detroit, Michigan 48202

New York Public Library
5th Avenue and 42nd Street
New York, NY 10018

Newberry Library
60 West Walton St.
Chicago, IL 60610

New England Historic Genealogical Society
101 Newbury St.
Boston, MA 02116-3087

The Civil War Library & Museum (GAR)
4728 Griscom Street
Philadelphia, PA 19124-3954

The Museum of the Confederacy
1201 E. Clay Street
Richmond, VA 23219

Chicago Historical Society
Clark Street at North Avenue
Chicago, IL 60614

Department of the Army
US Army Military Historic Institute
Carlisle Barrack, Bldg. 22
Carlisle, PA 17013-5008
carlisle-www.army.mil/usamhi/

Confederate Research Center
P.O. Box 619
Hillsboro, TX 76645

Department of the Navy
Navy Historical Center
Washington Navy Yard
Washington, D.C. 20374

Marine Corps Historical Center
Building 58
Washington Navy Yard
Washington D.C. 20374

Ladies of the Grand Army of the Republic
204 E. Sellers Ave
Ridley Park, PA 19078

Sons of Union Veterans of the Civil War
200 Washington Street, Suite 614
Wilmington, DE 19801

Daughters of Union Veterans of the Civil War
Library and Museum
503 S. Walnut
Springfield, IL 62704

Sons of Confederate Veterans
Elm Springs
Box 59
Columbia, TN 38401-0059

United Daughters of the Confederacy
P.O. Box 4868
Richmond, VA 23220

Federal Census of Union Veterans 1890

As part of the census of 1890, a special enumeration was taken of Union Veterans of the Civil War. The 1890 Census was partially destroyed by fire in 1921, but the Union Veteran Schedules are available on microfilm for states of Kentucky through Wyoming. The census films and the indexes are available through the National Archives and it's branch repositories, the Family History Library and Family History Centers, and major libraries and archives. The census indexes were produced by Index Publishing of Salt Lake, Utah or Accelerated Indexing Systems Inc. of North Salt Lake, Utah.

Questions on 1890 Census of Union Veterans *

> House number
>
> Family number
>
> Names of surviving soldiers, sailors, and marines, and widows
>
> Rank
>
> Company
>
> Name of Regiment or Vessel
>
> Date of Enlistment
>
> Date of Discharge
>
> Length of Service (Years, Months, Days)
>
> Post Office Address
>
> Disability Incurred
>
> Remarks

*1890 Census of Union Veterans *sometimes* listed a Confederate Veteran by mistake, then scratched out the information. This data is still sometimes legible. So, your Confederate Veteran *may* be accidentally listed.

Best Bet

Family Tree Maker, Family Archive # 131, Veterans' Schedules, U.S. Selected States, 1890. CD contains an index of approximately 385,00 war veterans and veterans' widows who were enumerated on the special veterans' schedule of the 1890 United States census. Although the

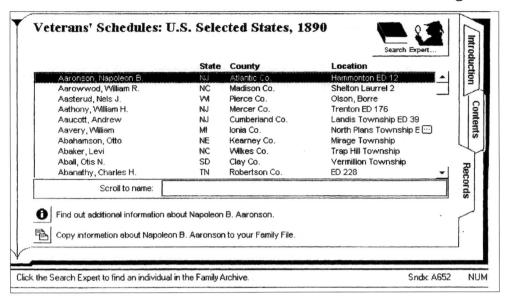

A sample page from Family Archive CD 131.

Veterans' Schedules: U.S. Selected States, 1890

Morbeck, Charles T.

State : MI
County : Menominee Co.
Location : Stephenson Township ED 90
Microfilm Page : 1

Morbeck, Rheinhard G. F.

State : WI
County : Manitowoc Co.
Location : Manitowoc ED 161
Microfilm Page : 2

Morcan, Edward

State : LA
County : Orleans Par.
Location : New Orleans
Microfilm Page : 105

Printed from Family Archive Viewer, CD 131 Veterans' schedules: U.S. Selected States, 1890, © The Learning Company, Inc.

1890 veterans' schedule was meant to record information on Union soldiers or their widows, it also lists some information about some Confederate soldiers. States represented include: AL, D.C., IL, KY, LA, MD, ME, MI, MS, MT, NC, ND, NE, NH, NJ, NM, NV, OK, OR, RI, SC, SD, TN, TX, UT, VA, VT, WA, WI, WV, and WY. There are a few from the states of CA, CT, DE, FL, GA, ID, IN, KS, MA, NY, OH, and PA. Please note that the state of Missouri is not included in this list of states.

Family History Library's Union Veterans Indexes to 1890 Census

STATE	INDEX AVAILABLE	FHL BOOK CALL NUMBER
District of Columbia	X	975.3 X22j 1890
Kentucky	X	976.9 X22d 1890 / fiche 6331355
Louisiana	X	976.3 X22l 1890; 976.3 X2d 1890
Maine	X	974.1 X22d 1890/ fiche 6331400
Maryland	X	975.2 X22d 1890
Massachusetts	X	974.4 X22d 1890
Michigan	X	977.4 X22d 1890
Minnesota	X	977.6 X22d 1890
Mississippi	X	976.2 X22d 1890; 976.2 X2j 1890
Missouri	X	977.8 X2d
Montana	X	978.6 X22j 1890
Nebraska	X	978.2 X2ja
Nevada	X	979.3 X22jv Index
New Hampshire	X	974.2 X22j 1890
New Jersey	X	974.9 X22j 1890
New Mexico	X	978.9 X22jv 1890
New York	X	974.7 X22dv 1890
North Carolina	X	975.6 X28j 1890
North Dakota	X	978.4 X22j 1890
Ohio		
Oklahoma	X	976.6 M2o; 976.6 X22ju1890

Oregon	X	979.5 X2j 1890
Pennsylvania		
Rhode Island	X	974.5 X22j 1890
South Carolina	X	975.7 X28j 1890
South Dakota	X	978.3 X22j
Tennessee	X	976.8 X2s 1890; 976.8 X2j 1890
Tennesseans in Texas	X	976.4 X2e 1890
Texas	X	976.4 X22dv 1890
Utah	X	979.2 X22jv 1890 index
Vermont	X	974.3 X22j 1890
Virginia	X	975.4 M2ju; 975.4 X22d 1890
Washington	X	979.7 X2j 1890
West Virginia	X	975.4 M2ju; 975.4 X22d 1890
Wisconsin	X	977.5 X22w 1890
Wyoming	X	978.7 X22j
US Misc. Army forts & prisons	X	973 X22jr 1890
US Vessels and Navy	X	973 X22j 1890

1890 Union Veterans Censuses Available*

STATE	NATIONAL ARCHIVES # M123	FHL MICROFILM #
Kentucky	M 123 rolls 1-3	338160 - 338162
Louisiana	M 123 rolls 4-5	338163 - 338164
Maine	M 123 rolls 6-7	338165 - 338166
Maryland	M 123 rolls 8-10	338167 - 338169
Massachusetts	M 123 rolls 11-16	338170 - 338175
Michigan	M 123 rolls 17-21	338176 - 338180
Minnesota	M 123 rolls 22-25	338181 - 338184
Mississippi	M 123 roll 26	338185
Missouri	M 123 rolls 27-34	338186 - 338192
Montana	M 123 roll 35	338194

Locating Union and Confederate Records

Eleventh Census of the United States.

Page No. _____
Supervisor's District No. _6_
Enumeration District No. _90_

SPECIAL SCHEDULE.

SURVIVING SOLDIERS, SAILORS, AND MARINES, AND WIDOWS, ETC.

Persons who served in the Army, Navy, and Marine Corps of the United States during the war of the rebellion (who are survivors), and widows of such persons, in _Stephenson Tp_ , County of _Menominee_ , State of _Michigan_ , enumerated in June, 1890.   _C. F. Fowler_ Enumerator.

From Schedule No. 1		NAMES OF SURVIVING SOLDIERS, SAILORS, AND MARINES, AND WIDOWS.	Rank.	Company.	Name of Regiment or Vessel.	Date of Enlistment.	Date of Discharge.	Length of Service.			
House No.	Family No.							Yrs.	Mos.	Days.	
1	2	3	4	5	6	7	8	9			
3	3	John Bruso		Private	H	20 Mis Inf	Aug 1862	Sep 1865	3	1		1
12	12	Morris Wm H.		Private	B	3 N.Y.S.A.	14 Aug 1861	July 1864	4	9		2
23	23	Hiram Corey		Private	G	24 Mis Inf	14 Aug 1862	17 July 1865	2	11		3
25	25	Manning John E.		Private	A	27 Mis Inf	21 Dec 1863	29 Aug 1865	1	8	9	4
30	31	Burley Ira		Corporal	D	16 N.Y.H.A.	17 Dec 1863	21 Aug 1865	1	8	3	5
38	39	Carley Wm A.		Private	G	16 N.Y.Inf	14 Feb 1861	12 July 1865		4	28	6
40	41	Morbeck Charles T.		Corporal	F	15 Mis Inf	22 Feb 1862	July 1865	3	1		7
42	43	Catharine Widow of Curley William		Private	I	6 N.Y.H.A.	23 1863	June 1865	1	6	8	8
58	60	Miller John B.		Private	G	5 Mis Inf	9 Feb 1862	10 Mch 1865	3		1	9
61	62	Larriviere Michael		Private	G	2 Mis Cav	14 Mch 1864	29 July 1865	1	4	15	10
61	63	Prickett Louis		Private	S	34 Mis Inf	1861	1864	3			11
			Private			186	186				12

POST-OFFICE ADDRESS.	DISABILITY INCURRED.	REMARKS.	
10	11	12	
Stephenson Mich			1
Ingalls Michigan			2
Ingalls Michigan			3
Ingalls Michigan	Vericose Ulcers	Walks with Crutches	4
Ingalls Michigan		Pioneer Corps Detached service	5
Ingalls Michigan		Shell wound above Ankle	6
Ingalls Michigan		Wounded by shell above ankle	7
Ingalls Michigan	Chronic Diarrhoea	Had rheumatism month	8
Ingalls Michigan			9
Ingalls Michigan			10
Ingalls Michigan			11
Ingalls Michigan	Injured spine, lame back	Fell from horse shot under him	12

Charles T. Morbeck Entry, 1890 U.S. Census, Veterans Schedule, Minominee County, Michigan, Stephenson township, ED 90 sheet 1; *National Archives micropublication M470, roll 21.*

Nebraska	M 123 rolls 36-38	338195 - 338197
Nevada	M 123 roll 39	338198
New Hampshire	M 123 roll 40	338199
New Jersey	M 123 rolls 41-43	338200 - 338202
New Mexico	M 123 roll 44	338203
New York	M 123 rolls 45-57	338204 - 338216
North Carolina	M 123 roll 58	338217
North Dakota	M 123 roll 59	338218
Ohio	M 123 rolls 60-75	338219 - 338234
Oklahoma and Indian Terr	M 123 roll 76	338235
Oregon	M 123 roll 77	338236
Pennsylvania	M 123 rolls 78-91	338237 - 338250
Rhode Island	M 123 roll 92	338251
South Carolina	M 123 roll 93	338252
South Dakota	M 123 roll 94	338353
Tennessee	M 123 rolls 95-98	338254 - 338257
Texas	M 123 rolls 99-102	338258 - 338261
Utah	M 123 roll 103	338262
US Vessels & Navy Yards	M 123 roll 104	338263
Vermont	M 123 roll 105	338264
Virginia	M 123 rolls 106-107	338265 - 338266
Washington	M 123 roll 108	338268
West Virginia	M 123 rolls 109-110	338268 - 338269
Wisconsin	M 123 rolls 111-116	338270 - 338275
Wyoming	M 123 rolls 117	338276
Washington, D.C., misc.	M 123 roll 118	338277

*To order HeritageQuest films or digital CD-ROM in Series M123 see chapter 22.

Federal Census of 1910

The 1910 Federal Population Schedule Census contains a column on the third column from the right side, that states whether a survivor of

Locating Union and Confederate Records

Kentucky, Breathitt County, 1910 U.S. Census, population schedule.
Micropublication T624, roll 466, Washington: National Archives.

Name.	Rank.	Co.	Reg't.	State or Vessel.	Post-Office.
Long, Jacob	Private	G	3	Wis. Cavalry	Platteville.
Long, Casper	do	G	46	Illinois	Browntown.
Long, William H	do	E	11	Indiana	Bruce.
Long, J. T	Corporal	G	16	Wisconsin	Downsville.
Long, Charles	Private	I	17	do	Prairie du Chien.
Long, Lewis	do	H	89	Indiana	Bon.
Long, Wm	Sergeant	G	3	Wis. Cavalry	Platteville
Long, W. H	Private	E	11	Indiana	Chippewa Falls.
Long, J. A	do	I	9	Indiana	Antigo.
Long, S. M	do	A	6	Wisconsin	La Valle.
Long, John	do	B	52	do	Leopols.
Long, E. J	Corporal	A	36	do	Buck Creek.
Long, George E	Private	K	87	Indiana	Connersville.
Long, Samuel	do	G	3	Wis. Cavalry	Platteville.
Long, Wm. H	do	H	25	Wisconsin	Potosi.
Longdo, Jos.	do	E	14	do	Bay Settlement.
Longe, August	do	E	49	do	Black Earth

Tabular Statement of the Census Enumeration, and Agricultural, Mineral and Manufacturing Interests of the State of Wisconsin, 1885. *Madison, Wisconsin: Democrat Printing Company, 1886, pg. 208.*

LEE COUNTY, ALABAMA, 1907 CENSUS OF CONFEDERATE SOLDIERS

145 - MILLS, Thomas J., present address Phenix, b. March 12, 1832 at Highlog in Montgomery Co., Ala., first entered the service as Private on June 15, 1861 at Fort Mitchell, Ala. in the Co. B. 15th Ala. and continued until close of war at Appomattox, Va.

146 - MILFORD, Alex Campbell, present address Opelika, b. Nov. 4, 1834 in Anderson Co., S. C., first entered the service as Private in April 1862 at Liberty, Ala. in the Co. K. 34th Ala. Regt. and continued until 4 months later. Re-enlisted as Private on Nov. 1864 at Opelika, Ala. in the Co. F. 8th Ala. Cav. and continued until close of war at Columbus.

147 - MONK, John, present address Smith's Station, Ala., b. Nov. 16, 1831 in Harris Co., Ga., first entered the service as Private in May 1862 at Opelika, Ala. in the Co. 1st. Bat. Hilliard's Legion and continued until close of war. Captured near Atlanta, discharged at Camp Douglass, Ill.

148 - MOORE, Burnett, present address Loachapoka, Ala., b. May 2, 1845 at Crawfordsville in Talliafers Co., Ga., first entered the service as Private on July 4, 1861 at Rome, Ga. in the Co. K. 38th Tenn. and continued until close of war, surrendered at Greensboro, N. C.

Alabama State Archives. Hale and Henry Counties, Alabama, 1907 Census of Confederate Soldiers. *Cullman, Alabama: The Gregath Company, 1983, pg. 41.*

Locating Union and Confederate Records

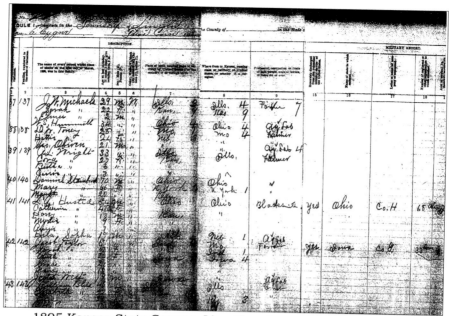

1895 Kansas State Census, Linn County, population schedule, Lincoln Township. *Family History Library, microfilm no. 570312, Salt Lake City, Utah.*

Louisiana State Archives. Enumeration of Ex-Confederate Soldiers and Widows of Deceased Soldiers, State Census of 1911, *Ascension Parish. Family History Library, microfilm no. 1412742.*

Union or Confederate Army or Navy. They use the abbreviations: *UA* for Union Army, *UN* for Union Navy, *CA* for Confederate Army, and *CN* for Confederate Navy. This is a means of finding if your soldier was on either side, is still alive, and where he is living for further possible pension information. The National Archives (T624), the Family History Library, and the HeritageQuest store (see chapter 22) have the Census films available. If using the Family History Library Locality Catalog lookup [STATE] - [CENSUS].

State Censuses Listing Civil War Information

State Censuses contain valuable information giving genealogical and military information on veteran soldiers, sometimes widows and orphans are included. Most of the State Censuses are available through the Family History Library as well as the State Archives. To find other censuses through the Family History Library Catalog lookup: [STATE] - CENSUS. Some of these films are available through the HeritageQuest store. See chapter 22 for ordering information.

STATE	CENSUS YEAR	CIVIL WAR INFO	RANK	NOTES	FHL FILM #
Alabama	1907	X			1421815
Alabama	1921 Conf.	X			
Arizona	1864		X		897437 item 5
Arkansas	1911 Conf.	X			fiche 6019335
Indiana	1886, 1890, 1894	X			1605057 starting number
Iowa	1885	X	X		1021316 starting number
Iowa	1895	X	X		1021706 starting number
Iowa	1915	X		Mexican War	1379445 starting number
Iowa	1925	X		Branch, Spanish, WWI	1429191 starting number
Kansas	1865	X		Regiment & Co.	570189-570198
Kansas	1885	X			975699 starting number
Kansas	1895	X			570221 starting number
Louisiana	1911 Conf.	X			1822969
Minnesota	1865	X			565714 starting number
Minnesota	1885	X			565733 starting number

Minnesota	1895	X		928767 starting number
Minnesota	1905	X	Mexican War	928767 starting number
New York	1865	X	Deaths of officers & enlisted men	see each county for film #'s
Oklahoma	1890	X		227282
South Dakota	1915	X	Mexican & Spanish	
South Dakota	1925	X	Spanish & WWI	
South Dakota	1935	X	Spanish & WWI	
South Dakota	1945	X	Spanish & WWI	
Wisconsin	1885	X		962237

Civil War Web Sites

The American Civil War	sunsite.utk.edu/civil-war/
American Civil War (Map Exhibits)	www.americancivilwar.com/civil.html
American Civil War Photograph Database	www.carlisle.army.mil/usamhi/PhotoDB.html
Ancestry Civil War Webpage (members only)	www.ancestry.com
A Barrel of Genealogy Links (Civil War)	cpcug.org/user/jlacombe/mark.html
Broadfoot Publishing Company (books, research services)	www.broadfootpublishing.com
Camp Life: Civil War Collections	www.cr.nps.gov/museum/
Civil War Research Database	www.civilwardata.com/
Civil War Soldiers & Sailors System	www.itd.nps.gov/cwss/index.html
Civil War Photos from Library of Congress	memory.loc.gov/ammem/cwphtml/
Civil War Prisons	geocities.com/soho/9787/cwprison.html
Civil War Reenactors	www.cwreenactors.com/
Civil War Regimental History Books	users.erols.com/jreb/regiment.html
Civil War Research	www.genealogy.com/7_morcvl.html
Civil War Web Sites	members.aol.com/Shortyhack/links.html
Confederate Regimental Histories Directory	www.tarleton.edu/~kjones/confeds.html
Cyndi's List of US Civil War	www.cyndisList.com/cw.htm
Daughters of Union Veterans	duvcw.org

Email Form 80, 85, 86 - Request (e-mail)	inquire@nara.gov
Grand Army of the Republic	www.nara.gov/genealogy/civilwar.html#GAR
Ladies of the GAR	www.rootsweb.com/~nlgar/home.html
National Archives–Civil War	www.nara.gov/genealogy/civilwar.html
Roots Web Civil War Mailing List	lists.rootsweb.com/index/other/Military/CIVIL-WAR.html
Roots Web Civil War Women Mailing List	lists.rootsweb.com/index/other/Military/Civil-WAR-WOMEN.html
Sons of Confederate Veterans	www.scv.org
Sons of Confederate Veterans	www.scv.org/
Sons of Union Veterans	suvcw.org/suv.htm
Union Regimental Histories Directory	www.tarleton.edu/~kjones/unions.html
United Daughters of the Confederacy	hqudc.org/
U.S. Civil War Center	www.cwc.lsu.edu/
U.S. Army History Institute	carlisle-www.army.mil/usamhi/
Valley of the Shadow: Living the Civil War in PA and VA	jefferson.village.virginia.edu/vshadow2/

Powder monkey by gun of *U.S.S. New Hampshire* off Charleston, S.C.
Library of Congress, Prints & Photographs Division (LC-B8171-4016)

21

Further Reading

Civil War

Groene, Bertram Hawthorn. *Tracing Your Civil War Ancestor*. New York, Ballantine Books, 1989.

Neagles, James C. *US Military Records, A Guide to Federal & State Sources*. Salt Lake City, Utah: Ancestry, 1994.

Katcher, Philip. *The Civil War Source Book*. New York: Facts on File, 1992.

Family History Library. *Research Outline*: *U.S. Military Records*. Edited by Ken Nelson. Salt Lake City: the library 1993.

Deputy, Marilyn; Roberts J.; Barben, Pat; Nelson, Ken; compiled by. *Register of Federal United States Military Records, Volume 2: The Civil War*. Bowie, MD: Heritage Books, 1986.

Nelson, Ken and Blalock, Marva. *Register of Federal United States Military Records, Volume 4, Supplemental*. Salt Lake, Utah: The Church of Later-day Saints, 1987.

Brown, Brian A. *In the Footsteps of the Blue and Gray: A Civil War Research Handbook*. Shawnee Mission, Kansas: Two Trails Genealogy Shop, 1996.

Union

Heitman, Francis B. *Historical Register and Dictionary of the United States Army 1789-1903.*, 2 volumes. Washington, DC: US Government Printing Office, 1903. (Officers)

Hewett, Janet B., editor. *The Roster of Union Soldiers.* 33 Volumes. Wilmington, NC: Broadfoot Publishing Company, 1998. (from Union Consolidated Military Service Records)

Munden, Kenneth W. and Beers, Henry Putney. *The Union, A Guide to Federal Archives Relating to the Civil War.* 1962 Reprint. Washington DC: National Archives and Records Administration, 1986.

Confederate

Beers, Henry Putney. *The Confederacy, A Guide to the Archives of the Government of the Confederate States of America.* 1968. Reprint. Washington, DC: National Archives and Records Administration, 1986.

Allen, Desmond Walls. *Where to Write for Confederate Pension Records.* 2nd edition. Bryant, Arkansas: Research Associates, 1994.

Crute, Joseph H., Jr. *Units of the Confederate States Army.* Midlothian, Virginia: Derwent Books, 1987.

Segars, J. H. *In Search of Confederate Ancestors: The Guide.* Atlanta, Georgia: Southern Heritage Press, 1996.

Neagles, James C. *Confederate Research Sources, A Guide to Archive Collections.* 2nd edition. Salt Lake City, Utah: Ancestry, 1997.

Hewett, Janet B., editor. *The Roster of Confederate Soldiers 1861-1865*. 16 volumes. Wilmington, NC: Broadfoot Publishing Company, 1996. (from Confederate Consolidate Service Records)

Krick, Robert K. *Lee's Colonels*. 4th edition. Dayton, Ohio: The Press of Morningside Bookshop, 1992. (Officers)

Brock, Robert Alonzo and Southern Historical Society. Southern *Historical Society Papers*. 52 volumes. Reprint. Wilmington, NC: Broadfoot Publishing Company, 1990-1992.

Robertson, James I., Jr., Editor. Index Guide to the *Southern Historical Society Papers 1876-1956*. 3 volumes. Wilmington, NC: Broadfoot Publishing Company, 1992.

Dornbusch, Charles E., Compiler. *Military Bibliography of the Civil War*. 3 volumes, 1961-72. Dayton, Ohio: The Press of Morningside Bookshop, 1987. (Union and Confederate)

Dyer, Frederick H. *Compendium of the Rebellion*. 2 volumes 1908. Reprint. Dayton, Ohio: The Press of Morningside Bookshop, 1978. (Union)

Sifakis, Stewart. *Compendium of the Confederate Armies*. 10 vols New York: Facts on File, 1992. (by state--Confederate)

Wright, John H., compiler. *Compendium of the Confederacy An Annotated Bibliography*. 2 volumes. Wilmington, North Carolina: Broadfoot Publishing Company, 1989.

Pensioners

US Pension Bureau. *List of Pensioners on the Roll, Jan 1, 1883*. 5 volumes. Reprint. Baltimore: Genealogical Publishing Company, 1970.

For Confederates: Family History Library Catalog search: [STATE] MILITARY RECORDS - CIVIL WAR - PENSIONS.

Cemeteries

Ramsey, Martha and William Ramsey, compilers. *Index to the Roll of Honor*. Baltimore: Genealogical Publishing Co., 1995. (Union burials during the Civil War)

Roll of Honor: Names of Soldiers Who Died in Defense of the American Union. 27 vols Washington DC: Government Printing Office, 1865-71.

Magazines

Confederate Veteran (Nashville, Tennessee). Confederate Veteran. 40 vols. Nashville, Tennessee: Confederate Veteran, 1893-1932.

Cumulative Index The Confederate Veteran Magazine, 1893-1932. 3 volumes, Wilmington, NC: Broadfoot Publishing Company, 1986.

In your local bookstore's Magazine Section:

America's Civil War

Civil War Times Illustrated, Editor: James P. Jushlan, A Primedia Publication, *North & South*, Editor: Keith Poulter, North & South Magazine, Inc.

Blue & Gray, Editor/Publisher: David E. Roth

Locating Union and Confederate Records

Washington, D.C. Officers at door of Seminary Hospital (formerly Georgetown Female Seminary), 30th St. at N, Georgetown. *1865 April. Library of Congress, Prints & Photographs Division (LC-B817-7875)*

22

HeritageQuest
Microfilm, Microfiche &
Compact Disk (CD)
Rental and Purchase

All microfilm, microfiche and compact disks (CDs) are available for purchase or loan and are listed in the twenty-four HeritageQuest specialty catalogs.

To order, select the items desired, note the call numbers and titles and call HeritageQuest toll free at 1-800-760-2455. You may also order online by accessing our Internet catalog at *www.HeritageQuest.com*.

Rental of Microfilm and Microfiche

The HeritageQuest microfilm and microfiche sets are available for rent by libraries, genealogical/historical societies and private individuals. Rental prices are available from the HeritageQuest sales clerks. Orders of ten or more rolls or sets of microfiche will receive a volume discount. Members of the Heritage Quest Research Club receive a membership discount. Rentals may be used for a period of one month. Renewals will be charged at the initial monthly rental rate, however, we recommend that if repeated renewals are required you purchase the items.

The price of renting microfilm rolls and microfiche sets may be applied to the applicable purchase price. Simply mark the shipping list, which came with the initial order as to the rental items that are desired for purchase. Enclose the shipping list or copy thereof along with the remaining monies (or credit card number) due to accomplish the purchase.

Rented items should be returned in the boxes in which they were shipped. The boxes are intended for repeated usage. Qualified organizations and individuals may ship the returns by Library Rate postage; others may use the Special Fourth class rates. A return-shipping label is included with the shipping list you received with the shipment.

Purchase of Microfilm, Microfiche and Compact Disk (CD)

All items held by HeritageQuest, with few exceptions, are available for direct purchase. Microfilm rolls come in two categories with the prices reflecting the type of microfilm. The most common is the diazo film which is a copy from a silver halide master film. The diazo films are coated with a special coating to resist wear and scratches. Silver halide copies may also be ordered at a higher cost. The silver halide films tend to show more detail than diazo copies.

HeritageQuest is currently scanning silver halide masters of microfilm and computer enhancing images when needed. These images are available for sale on compact disks (CDs). Usually the CD item number is the same as the roll number of the microfilm with an addition of "CD" to the beginning of the item number.

Satisfaction Guarantee

Quality of the film, fiche and CD copies, but not the original microform or material, is guaranteed by a 100% replacement policy.